EXPOSITORY ILLUMINATION

The Holy Spirit's Vital Role in Unveiling His Word

Jeffrey C. Crotts

Brian Overholtzer

KRESS
BIBLICAL
RESOURCES

For we do not preach ourselves but Christ Jesus as Lord, and ourselves as your bond-servants for Jesus' sake. For God, who said, "Light shall shine out of darkness," is the One who has shone in our hearts to give the Light of the knowledge of the glory of God in the face of Christ.
(2 Cor. 4:5—6, NASB)

CONTENTS

1

Introduction

Jeff Crotts

When I was seven, my family attended a small Baptist church, and my first memory of understanding illumination comes from the close of one particular service there. The congregation was singing "Turn Your Eyes upon Jesus" (Helen H. Lemmel), and these words from the chorus touched my tender young heart: "Turn your eyes upon Jesus/Look full in his wonderful face/And the things of earth will grow strangely dim/In the light of his glory and grace." I was moved, but I also understood that this "seeing" of Jesus meant something other than physically seeing him in front of me—it was a spiritual seeing. I understood this to be believing and seeing Jesus by faith—the essence of spiritual illumination.

Nearly a decade later, and as a newly converted teenager, I remember thinking through this concept again from a different vantage point. My family was now attending a different Baptist church, and I was challenged, in a way very similar to when I was seven, to think at the close of a service. We were ending our annual evangelistic concert, and I remember being stunned by something my worship pastor said. As was his custom, he concluded the event by making an appeal to those in attendance to believe in Jesus as their personal Savior. On this particular evening, instead of quoting a classic gospel passage like John 3:16 or Acts 16:31, he chose to paraphrase the French philosopher Blaise Pascal. Pascal said, "Belief is a wise wager ... faith cannot be proved, [so] what harm will come to you if you gamble on its truth and it proves false? If you gain, you gain all; if you lose, you lose nothing. Wager, then, without hesitation, that He exists."[1]

I was very young in the Lord, and hearing this from one of my pastors made me feel weak and kind of sick inside. What kind of Christianity was this man promoting? It appeared to me that he was presenting coming to Christ as some kind of gamble, and that he had no settled assurance. This approach seemed ridiculous to me, probably since I was such a new believer, had just been snatched out of a rebellious lifestyle, and was so keenly aware of the transformation that had taken place in my life. I was certain that I stood on a significantly more solid foundation than a mere philosophical gamble. I was not yet schooled in the doctrine of the Spirit, but I remember sitting in that service with a fundamental clarity over this issue and a deep assurance that God had made me his own and I was going to heaven. I knew that my conversion had been a work of God, not some kind of wager.

Twenty years later, I found myself face to face once again with the reality of illumination. As a pastor of a group of young adults, I was sitting in my office with a young couple, having an informal visit to get to know one another better. I wanted to hear from them how their dating relationship was going. I did not have an easy, natural way to break into conversation, so since I really did not know how these two were doing spiritually—or, to be honest, whether or not they were genuine believers—I decided to simply ask them to share their personal testimonies. What they began to share both surprised and humbled me, as they each, in their own words, connected their conversions to our young adults' Bible study of the previous summer, when I had taught a topical series on the theme of "godliness."

I was stunned. All I could think of while they were telling me of their conversions was how weak I thought my presentations of the Word had been that summer. Of course, I understood that God saves people by his grace, but my sermons had just been so bland! My content was biblical, and I was convinced of the truth of what I was saying; but I knew that at the time, I had felt that my teaching had not come off particularly well. As they spoke of their new growing relationships in the Lord, I listened gratefully, with a lump in my throat, and concluded one thing: the power that saved them was obviously not from me. The Apostle Paul summarized my experience perfectly when he wrote to the Corinthian believers, saying, "… my speech

---

[1] Blaise Pascal and W. F. Trotter, tr., *Pensées*, (New York: Random House, 1941)

and my message were not in plausible words of wisdom, but in demonstration of the Spirit and of power, that your faith might not rest in the wisdom of men but in the power of God" (1 Cor. 2:4–5). Paul knew that the power of God never came through slick communication skills, but rather by the Spirit of God. God is the one who saves, and the Spirit of God did his work through the Word of God.

A growing understanding of the significance of illumination has compelled me to search the Scriptures to better clarify and understand this biblical doctrine, and this study has been nothing less than amazing. Grasping this truth as it is laid out in the Bible has crystallized for me what occurred during my salvation as well as what my role is now as a pastor who communicates God's truth. In this aspect, my study has been quite liberating.

Understanding the role of the Holy Spirit in preaching has in some ways taken pressure off, and in other ways put more on. In terms of the act of preaching, I sense less pressure as I have come to recognize that it is up to the Holy Spirit to open people's spiritual eyes to the truths presented in a sermon. At the same time, this doctrine increased pressure for me as I began to understand how crucial it is to accurately interpret and present the Scriptures with the recognition that the instrument the Spirit uses to illumine people is his Word. Instead of placing the emphasis on great communication, my goal is to remove any obstacles that muddy the clarity of the truth I present so as to promote the Spirit's role of illumination.

Accountability has increased for me, not just as a preacher, but also as a Christian. I understand my need to have personal integrity to first seek God before seeking to be illumined in study. As a communicator, it is no longer sufficient for me to focus simply on right interpretation and preparation of a passage. I should never settle for mere accuracy—I must have the Holy Spirit's illumination. I need the Spirit first to illumine to my own heart the text I am planning to preach so that my own life may be transformed by my preaching preparation. This is a call for authenticity and personal integrity in the pastor's study. The words of my homiletics mentor from college still ring in my ears: "It is not how many times you go through the Word, but how many times the Word goes through you." My focus in sermonic preparation has become more God-centered.

I do not believe that this emphasis now gives me the excuse to be passive and say, "Well, since it is not up to my speaking ability, I will just coast through my sermon." Nor do I think I should remove all personality from my delivery, that a mark of being really deep or spiritual is to be boring in the pulpit. This emphasis, this call for illumination, raises the bar and sets a higher standard for the preparation process and delivery of the sermon. The challenge to be first illumined by the Spirit of God is the challenge to work more diligently, not only in the aspects of critical study and communication, but also in spending time in spiritual meditation on the text. I must engage with the passage on a heart level. A true understanding of illumination does not allow for sermon preparation to be solely academic, a merely perfunctory exercise. Instead, I must come to my study as a matter of personal sanctification, begging God and saying, "Open my eyes, that I may behold wondrous things out of your law" (Ps. 119:18).

Make no mistake—this adds pressure to the preparation. But isn't it worth it? Being illumined by the text before preaching it is truly the essence of being an authentic communicator. Often, those listening can sense when I have been affected by the text I am preaching. This not only makes for powerful preaching, it also models the very thing that I desire to see happen in the hearts of those who are hearing.

Brian Overholtzer

In the summer of 2019, my wife, her parents, and I drove up from Anchorage, Alaska to Denali National Park. Several memories were made that weekend which will stay with me for the rest of my life. From the eight grizzly bear sightings to the breathtaking view of Mount Denali on a clear summer day, we were blessed with the privilege to gaze our humble eyes upon what our Almighty God created. Out of all that my eyes beheld that weekend, one sight was most intriguing and got me thinking about the doctrine of illumination.

At 2am, the sky was lit up with dazzling rays of lights called the "aurora borealis" (also referred to as the northern lights). This wonderfully designed phenomenon is another sight to behold **God's glory in creation**. This phenomenon occurs when electrically charged particles originating from the sun collide with different gases in the earth's atmosphere. My wife, her parents, and I were very eager to see this sight! However, when they woke us up at 2am, I took too long looking for my shoes as I stumbled across the tiny room like a … well, a man who was woken up at 2am.

I frantically made my way outside, having given up on my shoe hunt, and I looked up into the dark Alaskan sky, and to my disdain, I saw some sort of cloudy outline, rather than a brilliant display of lights. My mother-in-law informed me that I missed the northern lights! In denial, I pointed at the shadowy figure and thought, "Wait, is that it?" Whatever it was, it looked intriguing, but there were no brilliant colors dancing and shooting across the sky. If I wanted to defend my position and claim that I did see the northern lights, I could appeal to scientific definitions and make the case that I saw a "toned down" display of the northern lights. Perhaps people would agree with me, or perhaps not. Whatever the verdict, one thing is clear—that the conversation would revolve around historical, literal, and measurable facts. A conversation would ensue filled with opinions, experiences, and frankly, a lot of subjectivity.

In the same way, many professing Christians and political activists today are making assertions about the gospel of Jesus Christ with much subjectivity. Furthermore, claims about the gospel are turning from opinions to redefining the gospel. Is the gospel as subjective as my experience of viewing the norther lights? Is the gospel open to interpretation beyond what is clearly said in Scripture? Is the culture's definition of justice a valid hermeneutical lens through which the gospel can be seen?

The answer is a resounding "No!" The biblical doctrine of illumination defends the gospel against those that would indirectly or directly attempt to re-define it. *Expository Illumination* guides the reader through the biblical doctrine of illumination as revealed by God the Spirit through Paul in 2 Corinthians 4:1–6. Supplementing these verses will be an array of Old and New Testament proof texts aiding to elucidate the prevalent occurrences of illumination in Scripture. Below is a synthesis of the meat of this book.

The doctrine of illumination spans the Scriptures. God has clearly spoken regarding the way in which he opens the minds of people to his Word. *Expository Illumination* will use four categories in order to organize scriptural references regarding the role of illumination:

Condemnation - referring to the person who is without illumination and is rejecting the Word of God.

Conversion - speaking of the transformation that takes place when God changes a heart and gives illumination.

Communication - speaking of how prophets, preachers, and evangelists are illumined to preach God's Word, and how hearers are illumined by the preaching of God's Word.

Convictions - which are gained as believers are enriched in their own spiritual walks, acquiring greater certainty and affection over spiritual truth as they are illumined by the Spirit and his Word.

2
A Synthesized Biblical Theology of Illumination
(2 Cor. 4:1–6)

The term "illumination," if looked up in a book about systematic theology, hermeneutics, or preaching, will typically have just a small section devoted to it, maybe only a simple definition of the work of the Spirit in the life of the believer. I was generally dissatisfied by the material available on the subject, and before beginning this study, I believed that much of what was written merely scratched the surface, especially in terms of living the Christian life. For me to be sure of this—to be convinced of its breadth and significance and to truly get a handle on what illumination is—I needed to comprehensively search the sixty-six books of the Bible to see what I would find.

So, I did. I used a standard Bible software program[2] and traced key words, words with either a direct or indirect bearing upon the Holy Spirit's work of illumining the minds of people, from Genesis to Revelation. Some of the words I surveyed were the following: spirit, spiritual, Holy Spirit, discern, perceive, discretion, witness, eye, ear, hear, taste, reveal, revelation, wisdom, knowledge, enlightening, light, meditate, and testimony. I then categorized them under their particular Bible books. This project turned into what amounts to a biblical theology, or a survey and analysis of this doctrine. I then analyzed each verse in its individual context, determining whether it contained a direct or indirect bearing upon this doctrine. This aspect of the

---

[2] BibleWorks 6: Software for Biblical Exegesis and Research, CD-ROM (Norfolk, VA: BibleWorks, LLC, 2005).

project became the meat of this book (the notes from my study can be found in Appendix II).

This study did not disappoint. I saw quickly that the doctrine of illumination spanned Scripture, and I was convinced that God had clearly revealed, in a variety of ways and in a variety of Bible books, that he illumines people with his Word. Four categories began to emerge as a way for me to classify these scriptural references regarding illumination. The first, condemnation, refers to the person who is without illumination, the one who is rejecting the Word of God. The second, conversion, speaks of the transformation that takes place when God transforms a heart by illumination. The third, communication, speaks of how prophets, preachers, and evangelists communicate God's Word, which is the means of illumination. The fourth, conviction, refers to the process whereby believers are enriched in their own spiritual walks as they gain certainty about biblical truth as the Spirit illumines the Word.

These four categories clarified for me that spiritual illumination is much more than simply knowing God more deeply by gaining new insights from studying the Bible. Spiritual growth is a part of the discussion of illumination, but its beginning point is salvation. Illumined people are genuine Christians; those without illumination are not. This is a serious doctrine. The Bible's teaching about illumination goes well beyond the idea of getting to know the Bible better; it shows that illumination has eternal consequences—spiritual life and death. The Bible draws a clear line—a person has either been illumined by the Holy Spirit or not, and, on this basis, is either growing in grace or not. I believe that it is because of the serious nature of this doctrine that it is woven throughout the entire biblical record.

Although I found these categories expressed throughout the whole of Scripture, I also discovered that they are crystallized in a single paragraph of the New Testament—2 Corinthians 4:1–6. No other passage in the entire Bible so succinctly captures these four themes of illumination, so I will briefly survey these verses in order to lay a foundation for this study. This way, the Scriptures serve as both the foundation and launching pad as we open up each category.

The Apostle Paul, author of 2 Corinthians, begins this particular passage by setting the stage, providing a context for his teaching on illumination. Here, as throughout the letter, Paul expresses his desire that this church clearly understand that his apostolic ministry is one of self-deprecation. He wants his readers to understand that he acknowledges the source of spiritual power for his ministry to be God, not himself.

EXAMINING THE CONTEXT

2 Cor. 4:1–2 *Therefore, having this ministry by the mercy of God, we do not lose heart. But we have renounced disgraceful, underhanded ways. We refuse to practice cunning or to tamper with God's word, but by the open statement of the truth we would commend ourselves to everyone's conscience in the sight of God.*

These lead-in verses clearly show that Paul gave all credit for his ministry in the life of this church to God. Essentially, he was labeling his preaching opportunity an undeserved gift. He called it a "ministry by the mercy of God." Paul never forgot who he was before he was rescued and transformed into a follower of Christ. This is one of many references to his pre-conversion state that Paul made throughout his writings. Reading Paul, one can sense that he never forgot how utterly lost and sinful he was before Christ called him to himself and saved him.

With this as his backdrop, Paul tells the Corinthians that he has a clear conscience—he knows that he has never manipulated his hearers as a gospel preacher. Where does this kind of humility come from? I believe that in Paul's case it came from his awareness not only of his past, but also of this essential work of spiritual illumination to the sinner which makes preaching effective.

Theme 1: Condemnation without Illumination

2 Cor. 4:3–4 *And even if our gospel is veiled, it is veiled to those who are perishing. In their case the god of this world has blinded the minds of the unbelievers, to keep them from seeing the light of the gospel of the glory of Christ, who is the image of God.*

Paul understood the Spirit's work of illumination, which gave him clarity about why people spurn the gospel. He did not blame himself or his preaching for their rejection, knowing that no matter how effective a communicator he was, no spiritual life could or would be produced apart from God's spiritual intervention. Here in verses 3 and 4, Paul puts the blame where it belongs. People reject truth because they are spiritually dead, because they are "perishing." He says that for those who are in this desperate spiritual state, the "gospel is veiled."

By saying this, he does not mean that people cannot physically read or hear gospel content, but that for them this message has been rendered insignificant, without value. Paul explains this in terms of Satan's soul-destroying influence, pointing out that "the god of this world" blinds people's minds.

Satan is a schemer and liar (John 8:44; Eph. 6:11) who is committed to facilitating gospel rejection by shrouding the Lord's saving light, keeping spiritually dead people dead. Perishing people are blind and unable to see and taste the glory and beauty of God that gives life to the soul through the work of the Spirit. To use a musical metaphor, it is as if, when the glorious gospel song is sung, Satan flips a distortion switch in the ears of the perishing so that the music sounds ugly, twisted, and unattractive.

Theme 2: Communication for Illumination

2 Cor. 4:5 *For what we proclaim is not ourselves, but Jesus Christ as Lord, with ourselves as your servants for Jesus' sake.*

Here, Paul communicates and emphasizes the content preached—"not ourselves," but one of the core truths of the gospel, "Jesus Christ as Lord." Since "Jesus Christ as Lord" is the essential message, this message is by nature authoritative. Paul makes it clear that it is this gospel message—not just any message—that transforms dead souls. The Apostle Peter calls the gospel the "imperishable" seed, the change-agent which germinates in the soul, causing life (1 Pet. 1:23). When this transformation takes place, Jesus reigns as Lord in the hearts of new believers. They are delivered from death's darkness and enlightened in their souls to see the face of Christ.

Not only is this message authoritative, but it is also communicated clearly, having no room for reinterpretation, opinion, or escape. Paul proclaimed the gospel, which is clear and authoritative because it came from God who has authority over all (Ps. 24:1; Eph. 1:22) and successfully communicates that which he intends. Since every word of Scripture is "God-breathed" (2 Tim. 3:16), it testifies to the clarity of the use of the word "gospel" found throughout its pages. For example, Scripture is profitable (vv. 16–17), it is addressed to common people (Eph. 1:1; 2:11; 1 Cor. 1:2, 26-31); additionally, parents can teach it (Deut. 6:6–7), and children can understand it (2 Tim. 3:14–15).

Theme 3: Conversion by Illumination

2 Cor. 4:6a *For God, who said, "Let light shine out of darkness," has shone in our hearts …*

Paul knew that it is no less a miracle for God to create spiritual light in a person who is "perishing" and "blinded" than for God to create the heavens and the earth from nothing. He clearly demonstrated that illumination is a creative event. When he wrote that God said, "Let light shine out of darkness," he referred all the way back to the beginning of time as documented in Genesis 1:1–3, where Moses wrote, "In the beginning, God created the heavens and the earth. The earth was without form and void, and darkness was over the face of the deep. And the Spirit of God was hovering over the face of the waters. And God said, 'Let there be light.'" This was not an allusion or vague reference to the creation event, but a direct comparison of spiritual conversion to physical creation.

Conversion is what takes place when people in a state of perishing come to know the glorious light of the gospel; it is the point at which God creates life in the otherwise spiritually dead and doomed soul. Conversion should be viewed as the beginning of illumination in a person's life. It is when they received the new birth and have therefore been born again. All things pertaining to this gift of illumination flow out of the creative event of conversion. Paul describes this spiritual transformation as the beginning, the source of all subsequent blessings, which we will refer to as the spiritual convictions gained throughout the Christian's experience.

Theme 4: Convictions Gained by Illumination

2 Cor. 4:6b ... *to give the light of the knowledge of the glory of God in the face of Jesus Christ.*

Paul depicts conversion as a saving event whereby a spiritually blind person experiences initial illumination—but he does not stop there. He goes on to speak of the fruit of conversion—the illumined convictions that he calls "knowledge." When he says that God gives "the light of the knowledge," he is not talking about bookish academic knowledge; rather, he is speaking of what a person in the deepest part of his or her being now affirms as unequivocally true. This person now possesses deep heartfelt certainty regarding biblical truth.

The "knowledge" or conviction of which Paul speaks is "of the glory of God," specifically "in the face of Jesus Christ." Obviously, he is not saying that newly illumined people physically see an image of the shining glorious Jesus Christ in their minds. Notice again how Paul uses the term "knowledge" to describe what happens in a person's soul. This person supernaturally gains something. He or she gains spiritual "knowledge"; he or she "knows the truth" (see John 8:32). In the case of 2 Corinthians 4:6, the believer is illumined to know, by conviction, that the glory of God is shining forth from the Son of God. Illumined believers see and taste glory because the Spirit has recalibrated their minds and affections to form a conviction that they have found the authentic Christ. They would stake their lives on it.

While a person receives illumined "knowledge" at conversion, the Bible also teaches that all believers should "grow in the grace and knowledge of our Lord and Savior Jesus Christ" (2 Pet. 3:18) throughout the entirety of his or her life (we will look at this more closely later in the context of Chapter 6). It is these illumined convictions that measure a person's relationship to Christ and spiritual maturity (2 Cor. 3:18; Col. 1:9–10).

I want to challenge the common perception that illumination is simply a way by which God enhances personal Bible study. These four categories reveal the weight and breadth of this doctrine. My hope is that these biblical truths will challenge and perhaps redefine the way the Christian life is understood, as well as the mission of the communicator of truth. For the preacher, meditation on biblical illumination may serve to open a window into the spiritual realm so that what is truly at stake in the preparation and preaching of God's Word becomes apparent. Let us see, with eyes spiritually aware, that those who are blind to the Spirit's illumination are condemned, that the communication of the gospel is the only hope a person has for being illumined, that when a person is initially illumined, his or her soul is actually being converted, and, once that person is converted, convictions are gained throughout the Christian life by means of illumination.

3

Condemnation without Illumination, Part I
(Old Testament)

2 Cor. 4:3–4 *And even if our gospel is veiled, it is veiled to those who are perishing. In their case the god of this world has blinded the minds of the unbelievers, to keep them from seeing the light of the gospel of the glory of Christ, who is the image of God.*

In order to understand what it means to be illumined by the Spirit; it is important to first understand why some are not illumined. Paul speaks of this when he says the "… gospel is veiled … [and] the god of this world has blinded the minds of the unbelievers …" (vv. 3–4). Unbelievers have a veil, or shroud of darkness, over their minds that spiritually blinds them to the truthfulness of the gospel. The unbeliever is powerless to see the glory of Christ. As we saw in Chapter 1, Paul specifically attributes this blindness to the god of this world, Satan, also known as "the prince of the power of the air" (Eph. 2:2). He is the one responsible for unbelievers being stupefied by and unable to spiritually apprehend the gospel (2 Cor. 4:4), thereby keeping them from turning to the Lord (3:16).

If God's sovereignty, his absolute rule (see Ps. 103:19; Rom. 8:28), is understood, then it follows that God is ultimately controlling and allowing for all things to take place. By implication, this means that God is permitting Satan to play this role of blocking the gospel. Why would God allow this? The future is so bleak for unbelievers. All who are without illumination are blind and presently under condemnation, and even on this side of eternity, they are already "perishing" (2 Cor. 4:3). This sounds as if it would be at cross-purposes with God's desire for mankind to be saved (2 Pet. 3:9), but is it really?

OLD TESTAMENT

Throughout the biblical record, God gives clear indication as to why so many are blind to the truth. A reading of the Old Testament shows that God's own chosen nation, Israel, was more often in spiritual darkness than in spiritual light. Israel's people and leaders ignored the prophets who warned them and instead ran after temporal lusts and the worship of false gods. The following Old Testament passages teach how Israel serves as an example of the blinding effects of sin and Satan on the minds of unbelievers in three ways: they were led by unqualified leaders, supported a sin-loving culture, and refused to confess their own personal sin-guilt.

A Former Word on Condemnation

One of these dark seasons of straying is documented in 1 Samuel 3:1, where one of the former prophets writes, "And the word of the LORD was rare in those days; there was no frequent vision." As the story goes, one of the reasons why God was withholding blessing was because of corruption in Israel's spiritual leadership, specifically in the leadership of the priesthood. Those who were expected to be most holy, those supposed to lead people to worship the one true God, were themselves ruled by their lust rather than by the Word of God. It wasn't God's revealed Word that guided their leadership and ministry, it was their own desires. The self-driven desires of unqualified leaders and their disobedience to God's Word led their followers into further condemnation.

The Blinding Effects of Unqualified Leaders

Serving as a bright contrast, Samuel was a faithful leader of God's Word, whom God called to service in the midst of a generation filled with unqualified and self-interest driven leaders. First Samuel 3:1 is the immediate backdrop to the story of Samuel's call. Think of how God called Samuel to serve as both priest and prophet in 1 Samuel 3. Remember how Samuel's mother, Hannah, had dedicated her son to be raised from infancy to be a priest? Samuel was living near the tabernacle, learning from his mentor, Eli, who, though he held the position of High Priest, had some serious parenting issues. Eli's sons, Hophni and Phinehas, were leaders in Israel, holding the position of priests. First Samuel 2:12–17 reveals the failures of their leadership, God's judgement of their leadership style, and the condemning impact their leadership had on the people they led.

To start the section off, the author describes Hophni and Phineas as "worthless" or "destructive"[3] men who did not know the LORD[4] (v. 12). Their actions in verses 13–15 demonstrate their labeling as religious leaders who were destructive and had no regard for the LORD. And these can be broken down into two groups: (1) Disregard for God's Word and (2) Disobedience to God's Word.

Disregard for God's Word

In Leviticus, God had instructed the priests how to conduct the "Fellowship Offering." In Samuel's day, the priests who ministered at the Tabernacle in Shiloh incorporated practices that were not part of those instructions that came from God's Word but instead embraced the customs of the people. Robert Bergen explains that "the priestly practices customary at Shiloh in matters of sacrifice are unlike those mentioned anywhere else in the Old Testament and clearly differ from those prescribed in the Torah (cf. Lev 10:14–15; Num 18:18)."[5] The priests of that time had little regard for the commands that came from Scripture. Hophni and Phineas joined in this deviation from God's Word. This deviation originated from a discontentment with God's Word, as Hophni and Phineas were "not content with the specified portions of the animals.... Eli's sons would take for themselves 'whatever the fork brought up ...'"[6] (1 Sam. 2:14). This is just one of the characteristics which led the Holy Spirit to move through the author of 1 Samuel to describe them as destructive leaders void of concern for God.

Disobedience to God's Word

Disregard for God's Word will always lead to disobeying God's Word. Hophni and Phineas' disregard for God's Word led them into direct disobedience of what God clearly directed in it. They disobeyed God by "taking the

---

[3] See the Excursus on the term "Belial," David Toshio Tsumura, *The First Book of Samuel*, New International Commentary on the Old Testament (Grand Rapids: Eerdmans, 2007), 122–124. For the translation "destructive," see Ibid., 154.

[4] The phrase "did not know the LORD" is not being used to describe their relationship with the LORD in terms of their sins being forgiven but refers to their regard for the LORD, see Tremper Longman III and David E. Garland, *1 Samuel–2 Kings*: The Expositor's Bible Commentary (Grand Rapids: Zondervan, 2009), 60. However, context does clearly articulate they were not "saved."

[5] Robert D. Bergen, *1, 2 Samuel*, vol. 7, New American Commentary (Nashville: B & H Publishers, 1996), 78–79.

[6] Tremper Longman III, "1 Samuel" in *The Expositor's Bible Commentary*, Rev. ed. (Grand Rapids: Zondervan Publishing House, 1992), 60.

priestly share of the fellowship offerings before the fat was burned"[7] (in violation of Lev. 3:3-5 and 7:30) and by "consuming the fat from the sacrificial animals (in violation of Lev. 7:22-26)."[8] Their disobedience was further manifested in their violent threats toward the people who questioned their authority to disobey God's instructions for leaders.

The Result: People Despise God

Actions have consequences. Especially severe are the consequences when a people are led by spiritual or religious leaders who do not regard God's Word and are destructive by ignoring it and disobeying it as well. The author of 1 Samuel summarizes the actions of these unqualified leaders, "Thus the sin of the young men was very great before the Lord, for the men despised the offering of the Lord" (1 Sam. 2:17).

Much of Old Testament narrative (such as the one we are currently reading) focuses on telling the story without commenting on the LORD's dissatisfaction toward great sins. However, on a few select occasions, the author, under the influence of the Holy Spirit, comments on the severity of the sin before the LORD. One well-known example occurs in 2 Samuel 11 when David commits adultery with Bathsheba and has her husband murdered upon discovering she was pregnant. The author remarks, "But the thing that David had done was evil in the sight of the LORD" (v. 27). Whenever an author takes the time to highlight the depth of a sin before the LORD, the reader should understand this notation to be expressing a significant theological point.

In 1 Samuel 2:17, we have one of these expressive theological points. The author, wanting the reader to understand the seriousness of their sins, says, "Thus the sin of the young men was very great before the LORD" (v. 17a), and following is the main reason for why this sin was so great against the LORD, "for the men despised the offering of the LORD (v. 17b). The Priests were entrusted with the responsibility to lead the people in worship. Their disregard for God's Word, and their disobedience toward it, led the people they were entrusted with to despise the worship service. This "despising" was more than a sneering at of the worship service; they disrespected the offering.[9] Such a result is shameful for anyone who would

---

[7] Bergen, *1, 2 Samuel*, 78–79.
[8] Ibid.
[9] "Disparage, disrespect," L. Ruppert, "נאץ," G. Johannes Botterweck, Helmer Ringgren, and Heinz-Josef Fabry, eds., Green, David E., tr., *Theological Dictionary of the Old Testament* (Grand Rapids; Cambridge: Eerdmans, 1998), 120.

lead people in worship. Sadly, the compromising of God's Word, causing the people to plunge further into darkness, was an issue in postexilic Israel, as is witnessed by Micah the Prophet.

God's Blessing of Dedicated Preachers

According to 1 Samuel 3:1, the patterns of sin in the lives of these leaders and the people they led meant that for the nation of Israel "… the word of the LORD was rare in those days; there was no frequent vision." God's people had their lifeline of communication with God severed. Hearing from God was rare. The satellite system was on the blink, and the television showed only snow. Though Samuel was stationed near the tabernacle, the place designed to be the center of the worship of the LORD, he too was bereft of God's fellowship because of the poor state of things, since "the word of the LORD had not yet been revealed to him" (v. 7).

Thankfully, the story does not end there. The LORD revealed himself to Samuel and did so while he was still a young boy. Upon hearing from God, Samuel declared himself to be the LORD's slave. He was now the one who "heard" God's Word (vv. 10–11). Later, he grew to be known not only as a priest but also as a prophet when, once again, "… the LORD revealed himself to Samuel at Shiloh by the word of the LORD" (v. 21). These revelations, first coming to Samuel and then ultimately to the nation through his prophetic ministry, changed the spiritual direction of Israel—God was again speaking to them.

From this narrative, it is apparent that sin is a barrier to illumination, especially when those who claim to be the spiritual leaders of the day are characterized by having no regard for God's revealed Word in Scripture and by disobeying the instructions from God written in Scripture. Though this seems obvious, it is nevertheless sobering and is a principle that can easily be forgotten. In 2 Corinthians 4, Satan is shown to be the blinder. Here in 1 Samuel 3, the root of the spiritual blindness is sin. The influences of Satan and sin form a biblical tension that comes up throughout Scripture (see Eph. 2:1–3; Jas. 4:1–7).

THE BLINDING EFFECT OF A SINFUL CULTURE

As we saw in the immediate backdrop of Samuel's call, Israel's spiritual leaders often led their people into rebellion against God and were sinful down to the bone. However, the rest of Israel are not off the hook. They were not simply victims of the sins of their leaders. The sins of the people shrouded the message that God gave to Israel. We are able to see this effect in the broader contextual background of 1 Samuel 1–7.

Key to understanding the contextual background to 1 Samuel 1–7 is the infamous book of Judges, where the larger contextual background of the passage takes place. Just recognizing that Samuel was born during the days of the Judges speaks volumes to the spiritual condition of the leaders and the people in his day. This negative background of Samuel's time is not just information that we know from comparing historical data. The author of 1 Samuel guides the reader to make several connections to the book and the time of the Judges. The better one understands Judges, the better one understands the days that Samuel lived in.

We have already run into an instance where the author points to Samuel's ministry during the time of the Judges. Earlier, we read in 1 Samuel 3:1, "And the word of the LORD was rare in those days; there was no frequent vision." This immediate background of "those days" was a time of the sinful leadership of Hophni and Phineas (1 Sam. 2:22–36). In 1 Samuel 3:1, the author guides the reader to the time of the Judges by making a direct allusion to the time of the book of Judges. The author accomplishes this with the intertextual use of the phrase "in those days."

Anyone who has read through the book of Judges would be able to identify the key verse of the book in 21:25: "In those days there was no king in Israel, everyone did what was right in his own eyes." Like the final statement in a long thesis paper, the author of Judges ends the book with this statement. He wants the audience to perceive the horrendous times of the Judges through the lenses of this statement. In fact, he repeats this statement a total of four times (Judg. 17:6; 18:1; 19:1 and 21:25) and uses those verses to frame the epilogue of the book.

After reading this phrase repeatedly, "In those days there was no king in Israel.... In those days there was no king in Israel.... In those days there was no king in Israel ..." you would say, "Ok, ok I get it, Israel was really bad and really needed a king." Hold on to that thought about Israel needing a king, it will come in handy in just a little bit. For now, we are immediately concerned about the rebellious state of Israel in the days of the Judges. The author makes this concern very clear by repeating this refrain four times, beginning it with the temporal phrase, "in those days."

We are concerned with Israel's rebellion and apostasy in Judges because the author of 1 Samuel has guided us to connect the time period of 1 Samuel with that of the Judges. This is not the only effort made by the author to direct the reader to understand the background of Samuel as the dark days of the Judges.

The circumstances of Samuel's birth are actually a direct parallel to Samson and the circumstances of his birth. In Judges 13:2, Samson's parents are introduced, "There was a certain man of Zorah, of the family of the Danites, whose name was Manoah; and his wife was barren and had borne no children." In 1 Samuel 1:1–2, Samuel's parents are introduced:

1 Sam. 1:1–2 *There was a certain man of Ramathaim-zophim of the hill country of Ephraim whose name was Elkanah the son of Jeroham, son of Elihu, son of Tohu, son of Zuph, an Ephrathite. He had two wives. The name of the one was Hannah, and the name of the other, Peninnah. And Peninnah had children, but Hannah had no children.*

Samuel is beginning to be presented as a sort of parallel to Samson. As we continue to read, we learn more about this connection.

A second parallel is seen between Judges 13:5 and 1 Samuel 1:11. In Judges 13:5, Samson's mother is instructed, "For behold, you shall conceive and give birth to a son, and no razor shall come upon his head, for the boy shall be a Nazirite to God from the womb; and he shall begin to deliver Israel from the hands of the Philistines." Compare this with Samuel's mother's words in 1 Samuel 1:11, "And she vowed a vow and said, ' Lord of hosts, if you will indeed look on the affliction of your servant and remember me and not forget your servant, but will give to your servant a son, then I will give him to the Lord all the days of his life, and no razor shall touch his head.'" Only two people in the entire Old Testament are recorded as being life-long participants of the Nazirite Vow— Samson and Samuel!

A third and final parallel between Samson and Samuel provides the full picture of the significance of Samuel's ministry in the dark times of those days. In this parallel, we will see that the failure of Samson in the days of the Judges is contrasted to the success of Samuel. There are many failures in the book of Judges. Samson's ultimate failure is that his sin and rebellion prevented him from fulfilling the purpose that the LORD had for him. "For behold, you shall conceive and give birth to a son, and no razor shall come upon his head, for the boy shall be a Nazirite to God from the womb; and he shall begin to deliver Israel from the hands of the Philistines" (Judg. 13:5). The LORD used Samson to begin the deliverance of Israel from the Philistines, but the LORD used Samuel to finish what Samson failed to do, as we see in 1 Samuel 7:

1 Sam. 7:3 *And Samuel said to all the house of Israel, "If you are returning to the Lord with all your heart, then put away the foreign gods and the Ashtaroth from among you and direct your heart to the Lord and serve him only, and he will deliver you out of the hand of the Philistines."*

1 Sam. 7:7–9 *Now when the Philistines heard that the people of Israel had gathered at Mizpah, the lords of the Philistines went up against Israel. And when the people of Israel heard of it, they were afraid of the Philistines. And the people of Israel said to Samuel, "Do not cease to cry out to the Lord our God for us, that he may save us from the hand of the Philistines." So Samuel took a nursing lamb and offered it as a whole burnt offering to the Lord . And Samuel cried out to the Lord for Israel, and the Lord answered him.*

1 Sam. 7:13 *So the Philistines were subdued and did not again enter the territory of Israel. And the hand of the Lord was against the Philistines all the days of Samuel.*

It was the ministry of Samuel in the dark time of the Judges that ended the darkness of those days. As stated earlier in this chapter, "sin is a barrier to illumination." How did God break the barrier of cascading sin in the time of the Judges? He raised up a man who listened to God's Word, pleaded with the people to follow God's Word, and led the people according to God's Word. It was the illuminating work of God's Word through the submission of a man to God's Word.

Corrupt Leaders and Unqualified Preachers

Hophni and Phineas are examples of Old Testament leaders that contemporary pastors should not follow. Regrettably, a devastating number of churches are shamelessly rushing such unqualified people into their pulpits. Men who have clearly not met the qualifications to be a pastor/elder, men who have disqualified themselves from their position or women who cannot every qualify to be a pastor/elder are being hailed as heroes of the day every time they take up the mantle of preacher.

This generation is screaming for women to peach, to especially disobey God's Word by taking on the office and or position of Pastor in clear violation of God's Word (1 Tim. 3:1–7). While many are open about their love for rebellion against God, there are those that claim to be unsure as to what God's Word really does say about the matter. It is at this point that an application of condemnation regarding women preaching is necessary. The first question to be answered in this application pertains to the perspicuity of Scripture. It answers the question, "Is God's Word clear?"

The Clarity of Scripture

Related closely to the biblical doctrine of illumination is the doctrine of the clarity of Scripture, also referred to as the perspicuity of Scripture. Illumination is the forensic (external) work of the Holy Spirit which enables a condemned person to believe God's Word. It must be stressed that "Illumination is not a work of the Spirit by which the Scriptures come alive in some subjective way to each believer. It does not provide new special revelation to the individual believer over and above what the text itself says."[10] Rather, illumination enables a condemned person to see and believe in the clearly communicated Word of God. A condemned and non-regenerate person can understand Scripture and can even write a thorough commentary on a book of the Bible or even write a systematic theology. This is due to the clarity of Scripture. At the end of the day, a person can only be illuminated by the power of the Holy Spirit who gives spiritual sight to the unregenerate so that they could believe what they formerly did not and could not. If such a person understood Scripture intellectually, then it was due to the clarity of Scripture.

The clarity of Scripture prevents people from adding or changing Scripture by means of interpreting it by their feelings, dreams, visions, or even by a claim to have been visited by Jesus himself. If someone claims to have an interpretation of Scripture that has not originated from the clear understanding of the reading and studying of God's Word, then that interpretation is to be discredited and exposed as originating from the person's imagination, sinful motives, or a combination of both.

Scripture Clarity on the Qualifications of Preachers

The first mistake of Hophni and Phineas was to disregard that which was already written in Scripture. There was a prescribed method to conduct the worship service, but their disregarding attitude led the people to destructive disobedience and being led away from worshiping God. Sadly, the same disregard and disobedience of God's Word is very prominent among so-called evangelical churches. This is specifically in reference to the increasing number of female pastors and those who claim female preachers are not only permitted in the Bible, but also encouraged.

---

[10] John MacArthur and Richard Mayhue, *Biblical Doctrine: A Systematic Summary of Bible Truth* (Wheaton, IL: Crossway, 2017), 104–5. Source not in bibliography.

The first issue to address is whether the Bible speaks on the issue, which it clearly does, commanding women not to preach. One of the clearest passages that contain this command is found in 1 Timothy 2:11-14:

1 Tim. 2:11–14 *Let a woman learn quietly with all submissiveness. I do not permit a woman to teach or to exercise authority over a man; rather, she is to remain quiet. For Adam was formed first, then Eve; and Adam was not deceived, but the woman was deceived and became a transgressor.*

This Scripture clearly prohibits women from "'teaching' (*didaskein* – διδάσκειν) and 'exercising authority' (*authentein* - αὐθεντεῖν) over a 'male' (*andros* - ἀνδρός)."[11] After reading such a clear and concise prohibition of women from exercising or holding the positions of pastors, elders, or teachers over God's people, it is astonishing that so many professing Christians disregard this passage and shamelessly disobey it.

Christians are clearly instructed in 1 Timothy 2:11-14 that women are prohibited from the role or function of being a pastor. This is not the only place where God has given instruction to his people on the standards for leadership in his church. Qualifications for the pastor-elder are clearly communicated in 1 Timothy 3:1–7 and Titus:

1 Tim. 3:1–7 *The saying is trustworthy: If anyone aspires to the office of **overseer**, **he** desires a noble task. Therefore an overseer must be above reproach, **the husband of one wife**, sober-minded, self-controlled, respectable, hospitable, able to teach, not a drunkard, not violent but gentle, not quarrelsome, not a lover of money. **He** must manage **his** own household well, with all dignity keeping **his** children submissive, for if someone does not know how to manage **his** own household, how will **he** care for God's church? **He** must not be a recent convert, or **he** may become puffed up with conceit and fall into the condemnation of the devil. Moreover, **he** must be well thought of by outsiders, so that **he** may not fall into disgrace, into the snare of the devil.*

Titus 1:5–9 *This is why I left you in Crete, so that you might put what remained into order, and appoint **elders** in every town as I directed you— if anyone is above reproach, the **husband of one wife**, and **his** children are believers and not open to the charge of debauchery or insubordination. For an **overseer**, as God's steward, must be above reproach. **He** must not be arrogant or quick-tempered or a drunkard or violent or greedy for gain, but hospitable, a lover of good, self-controlled, upright, holy, and disciplined. **He** must*

---

[11] William Varner, *To Preach or Not to Preach* (CreateSpace Independent Publishing Platform: 2018), 44.

hold firm to the trustworthy word as taught, so that **he** *may be able to give instruction in sound doctrine and also to rebuke those who contradict it.*

These passages are unmistakably clear. God has given clear instructions on the qualifications for the pastor-elder in his church. Disregarding these qualifications is blatant disobedience to God and is a sin. It should not shock the Christian that unbelievers are demanding churches to allow women to be pastors. They are not able to believe the truth of Scripture since they are unillumined and in a state of condemnation. Yet, there is a growing number of churches and other Christians who are encouraging and even demanding that women be pastors. Furthermore, when church leaders promote this agenda, they are instructing God's people that God's clear instruction on church leadership qualifications are either wrong or not relevant to the Christian today. When Christians are taught this by those whom God has supposedly entrusted with his Word, how will they trust any other instruction given by God? Is the command for men to not lust just as easy to disregard? There is no middle ground. Churches or Christians who compromise on God's truth are not acting like illumined believers.

A Word of Encouragement

For those who are reading this and are convicted by the Holy Spirit, please let me provide some encouragement. Our Lord is compassionate and merciful. I think about the many times in my life where the Holy Spirit has convicted me of sin from the clear and authoritative Word of God. Every single time, the Lord has been faithful to forgive me. I know he has forgiven me because of the clarity and sufficiency of His Word in 1 John:

1 John 2:1–6 *My little children, I am writing these things to you so that you may not sin. But if anyone does sin, we have an advocate with the Father, Jesus Christ the righteous. He is the propitiation for our sins, and not for ours only but also for the sins of the whole world. And by this we know that we have come to know him, if we keep his commandments. Whoever says "I know him" but does not keep his commandments is a liar, and the truth is not in him, but whoever keeps his word, in him truly the love of God is perfected. By this we may know that we are in him: whoever says he abides in him ought to walk in the same way in which he walked.*

The same clarity of Scripture that prohibits women from preaching and teaching in the church, is the same clarity of Scripture that ensures us of the faithfulness of Christ, our Advocate and great High Priest, to forgive us our sins. But this access to the Father through the Son is only available to those who "know him." Following this encouragement is a reminder that those who know him, keep his commandments. May we all work diligently to know his commandments and obey them with all our hearts.

A LATTER WORD ON CONDEMNATION

A second Old Testament book instructing on condemnation is found in one of the most impressive books among the Latter Prophets: the book of Isaiah. The theme of illumination and condemnation is interwoven throughout this marvelously written book. In the first chapter, Israel is charged, convicted, and condemned for their continual disobedience and rebellion against God's Word. One of their condemnations was for not having illumination, "Israel does not know, my people do not understand" (Is. 1:3b). The reality of their lack of illumination is repeated in the second half of the book, "They do not know, nor do they understand, for He has smeared over their eyes so that they cannot see and their hearts so that they cannot comprehend. No one recalls, nor is there knowledge or understanding ..." (44:18-19b). Significantly, the Servant of the LORD is revealed to be the One who is endued with the Spirit of wisdom and understanding (11:1-10; see also 4:2-6; 9:1-7; 32:1-20; 40-66). Amazingly, these don't even cover all the instances of illumination that occur in Isaiah. Surely, we can learn a lot from Isaiah on the doctrine of illumination. Our attention is drawn toward two texts: Isaiah 6 and 1; both concerned with the condemning state of the unillumined.

Condemnation according to Isaiah

Remember when the LORD called Isaiah into prophetic ministry? Isaiah was the LORD's spokesman during some of Israel's most unholy days. Before he could minister to God's people, there was an issue that needed resolution. Isaiah was not qualified to preach because he was a condemned sinner. Isaiah 6 reveals three realities surrounding the prophet before he was summoned to ministry.

Verse 1 recounts that Judah's king Uzziah died, and Isaiah went into the temple to seek the LORD on behalf of the nation. In a moment, Isaiah was swept up into a heavenly vision, in which he saw the exalted LORD. Surrounding the exalted LORD were fiery angels (Seraphim) who had six wings each: two wings to cover their face to protect them from gazing upon the magnificent holiness of the LORD, two wings to fly in order to keep a safe distance from the holiness of the LORD and two wings to cover their feet, further demonstrating their posture of humility before the high and exalted King of Holiness. It is to no surprise that they called out in praise, proclaiming, "Holy, holy, holy is the LORD of Hosts!"

Isaiah had no wings to protect him from the magnificence glory of the LORD. He was in a dangerous situation since the LORD told Moses in Exodus 33:20, "you cannot see my face, for man shall not see me and live" This reality is due to man's fallen condition. Man was first separated from the LORD in Genesis 3 after Adam sinned. Adam was removed from the presence of the LORD, and mankind has been separated from him ever since. As a condemned man born from the line of Adam, he was before the presence of the holy God.

Guilt That Condemns

Suddenly, being in God's holy presence crushed him with guilt and despair. The passage describes Isaiah as feeling completely "lost," or, more literally, as if he was disintegrating or ceasing to exist. Isaiah saw no hope for restoration in his self-pronounced "woe" judgment, which meant he understood himself to be condemned (Is. 6:5). He confessed, "I am a man of unclean lips, and I dwell in the midst of a people of unclean lips." Israel had unclean lips—that is, they were guilty of sin that separated them from the LORD. How could a guilty person be sent to minister to a guilty people? You don't send a blind person to walk another blind person across the street. Isaiah was certainly not qualified or equipped to represent any message of the LORD with such a guilty verdict on his shoulders.

Sacrifice That Cleanses Condemnation

After Isaiah's confession of his sin-guilt, an angel flew to him, touched his lips with a burning coal that had been taken from the altar, and declared to him that his iniquity was taken away and his sin was forgiven (v. 7). Isaiah was no longer a condemned man. It was only after having his sins atoned for that he could have his relationship with the LORD restored. In his case, the LORD granted grace, honoring his contrite response not merely by restoring him, but also by issuing a call for him to preach. Without hesitation, Isaiah accepted (v. 8).

Isaiah's Ministry Call: Preach Condemnation

The picture of a man of God signing up to preach for God is not new or unusual. What is striking here is the goal God set for Isaiah's ministry. His primary ministry objective was not pretty. The LORD assigned this preacher the task of being a messenger who, for the most part, would always be rejected. His gospel ministry would mostly result in death, not life. In other words, he preached for the purpose of condemnation. When Isaiah first heard God's summary of what his preaching ministry was going to be like, it must have been discouraging:

Is. 6:9–10 *And he said, "Go, and say to this people: 'Keep on hearing, but do not understand; keep on seeing, but do not perceive.' Make the heart of this people dull, and their ears heavy, and blind their eyes; lest they see with their eyes, and hear with their ears, and understand with their hearts, and turn and be healed."*

Anyone hearing this call would be tempted to say, "Wait a minute, I'm not sure what I just agreed to do." Isaiah's preaching was first and foremost a ministry of condemnation—preaching to cause spiritual blindness. This is not the reason why preachers usually go to seminary. Keep in mind the core issue, though. People are born in sin, and their rejection of God warrants condemnation. It was for this purpose that Isaiah was commissioned to preach.

While Isaiah records his commissioning in chapter 6, his message starts in chapter 1. Isaiah's introductory chapter provides the broad backdrop of condemnation in Isaiah. A backdrop which expands over the entirety of the 66 chapters of the book! Conveniently, chapter 1 contains a summary of all the themes of the book—including condemnation. Isaiah's first message of condemnation in occurs in 1:1-15.

In chapter 6, Isaiah himself is shown to be guilty for his own sins, and he briefly mentions the guilt of the people he lives among. In Isaiah 1:1-15, the guilt of the people is explained in more detail. In this prophetic lawsuit against the corporate people of God, the individual is condemned because he or she has sinned against the Holy One of Israel. It is this theme which runs predominantly through the first major half of Isaiah (chapters 1-39), setting up for the dramatic shift for the first words in chapter 40, which begin with "Comfort, comfort my people, says your God." Before the good news, there must be an accurate communication of condemnation, a message which the LORD reveals through the prophet Isaiah with unobstructed clarity.

The Condemnation of Israel's Sin Guilt: Isaiah 1

Among evangelical discussions, the topic of corporate guilt and corporate repentance is hotly debated, and is gaining attention exponentially. Few chapters in the Bible address corporate guilt more clearly than in this introductory chapter of Isaiah.

Isaiah quickly introduces himself in the first verse of the book and immediately gets to the point that sinful Israel is guilty before their holy God starting in verse 2. He communicates this condemning reality for Israel using the common literary genre of a "prophetic lawsuit."[12] Reading the text through the lens of Israel on trial is not only helpful and engaging, but is also the intended method by the author. The following chart is a summary of the prophet's message of condemnation against Israel in Isaiah 1:1-20.[13]

1. The heavens and earth are called as witnesses (cf. vv. 2–3).

2. Israel is accused of sin, disobedience and rebellion (cf. vv. 4–6).

3. The LORD's patience is contrasted with Israel's continual rejection of his mercy (cf. vv. 7–9).

4. Israel's false worship as a means to atone for the guilt of their sins is rejected (cf. vv. 10–15).

5. The LORD offers a final ultimatum to solve Israel's condition and position of guilt (cf. vv. 16–20).

Just as there were three lessons of condemnation surrounding Isaiah's call to ministry in chapter 6, there are three lessons that encompass Isaiah's message of condemnation against Israel.

The Holy One Who Condemns: Isaiah 1:4

The LORD as the Holy One of Israel is a central theme in Isaiah. John Oswalt elaborates on how Isaiah evenly interweaves the phrase, "the Holy one of Israel," (twelve occurrences in chapters 1-39; thirteen in chapters 40-55)."[14] Its first occurrence is within Isaiah's first message of condemnation:

Is. 1:4 They *have forsaken the Lord, they have despised the Holy One of Israel, they are utterly estranged.*

---

[12] David A. Dorsey, *The Literary Structure of the Old Testament: A Commentary on Genesis–Malachi* (Grand Rapids: Baker Academic, 1999), 218.

[13] This list is from D. Brent Sandy and Ronald L. Giese, Jr., eds., *Cracking Old Testament Codes* (Nashville: B & H Publishers, 1995), 163.

[14] John Oswalt, *The Holy One of Israel* (Eugene, OR: Wipf and Stock Publishers, 2014), 3.

The Depth of Israel's Condemnation: Isaiah 1:4–9

Isaiah confessed his own guilt when he was before the overwhelming presence of the Holy One of Israel (6:5). He was also very aware of the guilt of the people he lived among. He cried out that he was a man of unclean lips and that he lived among a people of unclean lips. Unfortunately, Israel does not cry out and confess their sins in Isaiah 1. Rather, they are accused of rebelling against the LORD (vv. 4-6), resisting the LORD's attempt to discipline them back to obedience (vv. 7-9), and attempting to hide their blood-stained hands under the cloak of external religious rituals (vv. 10-15).

These accusations reveal several important aspects of Israel's condemnation. First, Israel was condemned for disobeying God's commands. The first words of Isaiah's message against Israel, "List O Heavens and hear O Earth" hearken back to Deuteronomy 31, where the LORD warned Israel that if they disobeyed his laws, the heavens and earth would testify against them. The summoning of the heavens and the earth to testify against Israel in Isaiah 1 is because Israel was disobeying God's laws and commandments.

Secondly, Israel's condemnation involved being compared to Sodom and Gomorrah. Sodom and Gomorrah were cities that the LORD condemned, judged and destroyed by raining down fire and brimstone on them (Gen. 19:24). The narrative of Genesis 19 portrays their great evil by highlighting the men of the city wanting to have sexual intercourse with the men that were with Lot and his family (v. 5). The depth of Israel's guilt is as the guilt and condemnation that was against the evil cities of Sodom and Gomorrah, who were characterized by the sin of homosexuality. Consider Isaiah's first message of condemnation, "They have forsaken the Lord, they have despised the Holy One of Israel, they are utterly estranged." (Is. 1:4).

The Breadth of Israel's Condemnation: Isaiah 1:10–15

Lastly, the breadth of Israel's condemnation is portrayed as guilt that must be resolved. Israel attempted to deal with their sins on their own terms. This included a reliance on observing the religious ordinances that were given to Israel. These took the form of sabbaths, festivals and assemblies. However, Isaiah informs Israel that relying on these external religious practices cannot resolve Israel's condemnation.

While these religious ceremonies are unrelatable to the majority of Americans today, one can imagine that Isaiah was talking to a church member who attended every Sunday morning and evening service. Imagine that he or she taught children's ministry every Wednesday night, prayed before every meal, and boldly stretched out his or her arms to the sky during worship services. According to Isaiah, this person was still condemned. His reasoning is simply that, "your hands are filled with blood" (1:15). This did not mean that only murderers were condemned. The Hebrew form of the word "blood" in verse 15 refers to the guilt of blood spilt by violence. This same Hebrew word form was used in Genesis 4:10 for Abel's blood that cried to the LORD from the ground. Israel's guilt was as severe as the guilt of murder. Left to themselves, they would surely be doomed to remain condemned under the breadth of their guilt and face the full wrath of the Holy One of Israel. Those condemned with this guilt are the inhabitants of Judah and Jerusalem (Is. 1:2) who have rebelled by turning away from God's laws in disobedience (v. 4).

Despite Israel's sinful nature and rebellious disposition, the LORD promised and provided cleansing by a sacrifice. This sacrifice is revealed immanently through the book of Isaiah, beginning in Isaiah 1:6-18, elucidated more in chapter 6, and it reaches a pinnacle in Isaiah 52:13–53:16—the great Servant Song. What can wash away my sin? For this cleansing what do I see? Surely, nothing but the blood of Jesus!

JUSTICE ACCORDING TO JONAH

Isaiah was given the task to preach a message of condemnation to Israel. Jonah was given a similar commission; except he was to bring a message to the Gentiles. These two prophets stand is stark contrast to one another, as the former faithfully carried out his task of crying out against a sinful and unjust people (Is. 58:1-2), and the latter fled from the LORD's mandate. Both of these prophets preached a message of condemnation. Throughout the book of Jonah, the prophet's version of justice runs in contradistinction with God's justice.

The Gospel according to Jonah

The LORD's heart and desire for all the nations is a theme which permeates throughout Scripture. In Genesis 12:3 and Exodus 19, it was made clear that Israel was given the significant task to be a mediator between God and the nations. Israel was not given the command to "go" as Christians are in Matthew 28:19-20, but was to be a sort of stationary missionary-like people. The LORD's commission to Jonah was slightly different than what prophets were told to do, but it was well within the heart of God's plan for the nations. Jonah's disdain for these oppressive Gentiles becomes evident in his fleeing to Tarshish after the LORD commanded him to go and preach to Nineveh.

Jonah's detestation against the oppressive Ninevites wasn't merely a re-fusal to go on a humanitarian aid missions trip. The prophet was commis-sioned by the LORD to bring a message of condemnation and repentance. Jonah was commanded to literally cry out against this nation and their sins against the LORD (Jonah 1:2). What exactly was Jonah to cry out? A surface reading of the phrase "to cry out" may seem vague. A parallel use of this word occurs in Isaiah 58:2 and helpfully sheds light on its meaning here. Less than a hundred years after Jonah, the LORD commanded Isaiah to cry out against Israel for their injustice and oppression and intended for this crying out to lead to repentance and restoration:

Is. 58:1, 8 *Cry aloud; do not hold back; lift up your voice like a trumpet; declare to my people their transgression, to the house of Jacob their sins.... Then shall your light break forth like the dawn, and your healing shall spring up speedily; your righteousness shall go before you; the glory of the LORD shall be your rear guard.*

Jonah preached during the reign of Jeroboam II, son of Joash (2 Kings 12:24-25). Jeroboam is described as an evil, wicked, and unjust king. Jonah would have most likely proclaimed messages of condemnation and repent-ance during this time. It was part of the job description. One of the messages that Jonah preached was that the LORD would restore a significant portion of the land to them.

Jonah seems to have happily preached a message of hope to his own people who were being afflicted by oppressive nations. But when he is com-missioned to take this message of justice and mercy to the people group that are the oppressors, he flees the occasion. Jonah strikes down the gavel to declare them guilty without hope. Jonah's justice was one which showed mercy to the oppressed people group and detestation toward the oppressors.

The World's Disdain toward Oppressors

A worldly view of justice celebrates and encourages Jonah's view of jus-tice toward an oppressive people group. Throughout history, the belittling of oppressive people has been applauded. Approval for taking human venge-ance against oppressive people can be traced as far back as Lamech in Gen-esis 4:23-24. The early descendant from the line of Adam boasts of his self-proclaimed act of retribution against those who had oppressed him.

Gen. 4:23–24 *Lamech said to his wives: "Adah and Zillah, hear my voice; you wives of Lamech, listen to what I say: I have killed a man for wounding me, a young man for striking me. If Cain's revenge is sevenfold, then Lamech's is seventy-sevenfold."*

While it is difficult to discern it in English, Lamech actually wrote this as a song. Lamech sang a song to his two wives, boasting that he took vengeance on a man and a boy who had offended him. Lamech's explanation about being avenged seventy-sevenfold compounds the extent to which he celebrates the retribution he enacted for himself.

Christ Confronts Pseudo-Justice

Jesus criticized such man-centered approaches to justice, and he used the Law to properly instruct his people on how they are to apply justice to those who oppress them. During antiquity, the Jewish religious leaders grossly misinterpreted the Old Testament and especially the Law (the first five books of the Bible: Genesis–Deuteronomy). While these Jews were "experts" in the Law, they were ignorant of its intended purpose. Jesus spoke of this purpose in Matthew 22:36-40, when one of the Pharisees asked him which was the greatest commandment, to which Jesus replied,

Matt. 22:37–40 *You shall love the Lord your God with all your heart and with all your soul and with all your mind. This is the great and first commandment. And a second is like it: You shall love your neighbor as yourself. On these two commandments depend all the Law and the Prophets.*

The Law can be mistaken for a book that is only about a lot of rules and stipulations. Jesus knew this wasn't the case; he knew his Old Testament well and simply told the Pharisee what the entire purpose of the Law was. The Law was meant to point us to loving God and loving others, and the book of Deuteronomy, the capstone to the Law, speaks more about the heart and loving God and others than any other book of the Bible. The theme of loving God encapsulates the Law.

In Matthew 5:38-39, Jesus makes it clear that upholding justice toward an oppressive person is not incompatible with the commands to love God and others. In a series of "You have heard it said … but I say to you …" statements, Jesus brings to light the different ways in which the Jewish religious rulers mishandled God's Law and corrected it with the actual meaning of the text. It appears as if the Jewish leaders were using the retribution law for justice found in Deuteronomy 19:21 in some kind of negligent manner. What might this incorrect manner be? The retribution law quoted by Jesus "an eye for eye" is actually a direct quote from Deuteronomy. Even when you read the text, it seems to be clearly stating the rules and laws for retribution when one person is oppressed by another. Is Jesus re-interpreting the Old Testament, is there a hidden truth in the Old Testament that was unknown to the people it was written to? Neither is the case. Jesus made sure that the whole point of the Law—loving God and loving others—was included in the law of retribution. To not connect love and mercy to the oppressor is to miss the whole point of the Law.

Demanding retribution for an oppressor without a thought to loving the oppressor is incompatible to God's definition of justice. Such a justice is man-centered and unbecoming to a Christian. A Christian's response to injustice and to oppressors must be in line with what Christ commanded. We must turn the other cheek, give the extra cloak, and go the extra mile. We must love the oppressor and at the same time not compromise on God's standards of righteousness and holiness. A departure on either end will result in a theological obscurity of biblical justice. While we travel through this combative and often oppressive world, may we remember that we must not only wish justice on those who persecute us, but we must also have a heart for our oppressors as well; otherwise, we might find that we too understand justice according to Jonah.

Conclusion

In 1 Samuel, we witnessed the effects of unqualified leadership on a sin-loving culture in a time when God's Word was rare. In Isaiah, we observed the prophet confronting a sin-loving culture that tried to hide their condemnation under the blanket of their religious practices. In Jonah, we perceived that the missionary-prophet desired the condemnation of a nation who had oppressed his people. We find the doctrine of condemnation before illumination permeating the Old Testament, and we will now examine it in the New Testament.

4

Condemnation without Illumination, Part II
(New Testament)

2 Cor. 4:4 *In their case the god of this world has blinded the minds of the unbelievers, to keep them from seeing the light of the gospel of the glory of Christ, who is the image of God.*

This theme of condemnation does not end with the Old Testament. In fact, because God's revelation became clearer and brighter with Jesus's coming, the condemnation also became more severe in the New Testament. The message of condemnation in the New Testament was the same message of condemnation preached in the Old Testament. Jesus did not come to abolish the Law, but to fulfill it (Matt. 5:17). The following New Testament passages capture how Christ and his apostles stand in a long line of prophets and preachers proclaiming the same message of condemnation from Moses to Malachi. They preached to a condemned people, pleading with them to confess their sins and to repent.

Jesus proclaimed the good news that he himself came to save condemned people from their sins. Condemnation is integral to the gospel message found in the written account of the good news concerning Jesus Christ, the Son of God. In the Gospel accounts of Matthew, Mark, Luke, and John, Christ relentlessly pronounces judgement. Throughout Jesus's ministry, he called for people to respond to his teaching, saying, "He who has ears to hear, let him hear" (Matt. 11:15). This was his way of distinguishing those who were spiritually illumined to hear God's Word from those who were not.

Many have wondered why, when Jesus taught parables, most of his hearers did not have the first clue what he was talking about. Why did Jesus so often teach this way? Was he trying to make spiritual truths easier to understand through stories? If so, why did so many people either miss or reject the point? Jesus's parables were not merely teaching tools, but also served as a condemnation of those who were spiritually blind. In this way, the parables were exclusively received by those who were illumined to understand them.

For those who would receive the light of Christ, the message of condemnation was actually good news. In this chapter, we are going to encounter the good news about condemnation and note the deceitfulness of what I call "false illumination."

THE GOOD NEWS ABOUT CONDEMNATION

In a moment, shepherds keeping watch over their flocks in the night were met by two fear-striking events followed by a gospel proclamation (Luke 2:8-12). One of these alarming incidents was the appearance of an angel of the Lord, and the other was being surrounded by the LORD's illuminating glory. In this instance, illumination is ascribed as striking fear into the hearts of these unsuspecting shepherds. When analyzing this astounding appearance of the Lord's glory, the word describing the illuminating glory (i.e., shone) stands out as unique among New Testament usage. The passage reads:

Luke 2:9 *And an angel of the Lord appeared to them, and the glory of the Lord shone around them, and they were filled with great fear.*

While the angel of the Lord suddenly appears, certainly a frightening experience, the Lord's glory is given prominence as an overwhelming and dreadful experience. How is it that God's glory shines and causes fear at the same time? The word translated "shone" is the Greek word "περιέλαμψεν" which a standard lexicon defines as "shine around." This accounts for the translation that the Lord's glory "shone around them." This is no ordinary word for shining. The root of the word is "λαμπω," which has the general meaning "to shine." This word occurs throughout the New Testament and has the semantic meaning of "shining". The word in Luke 2:9 occurs with the prefixed preposition "περι," intensifying the verb.

The NLT brings out this strengthening: "the radiance of the Lord's glory surrounded them." This overwhelming brilliance is not a novel experience in Scripture. Clinton E. Arnold recalls that, "The 'glory of the Lord' is God's visible presence in creation and is associated with awesome events in Israel's past: the giving of manna (Exod. 16:10) and the covenant at Sinai

(24:16–17)."[15] Moses provides a detailed account of what this brilliant display of the Lord's overwhelming glory was like:

Exodus 24:16–17 *The glory of the LORD dwelt on Mount Sinai, and the cloud covered it six days. And on the seventh day he called to Moses out of the midst of the cloud. Now the appearance of the glory of the LORD was like a devouring fire on the top of the mountain in the sight of the people of Israel.*

Furthermore, the verb used to describe the brilliant display of the Lord's glory is used only one other time in the New Testament—on the Damascus Road. Paul recounts this encounter:

Acts 26:12–14 *In this connection I journeyed to Damascus.... At midday, O king, I saw on the way a light from heaven, brighter than the sun, that shone around me and those who journeyed with me. And when we had all fallen to the ground, I heard a voice saying to me in the Hebrew language, "Saul, Saul, why are you persecuting me?"*

Saul's encounter with Christ's illuminating glory on the road to Damascus was a gospel moment for him. His life was transformed by the good news of Christ. Likewise, in Luke 2:8-14, the announcement of Christ's birth is proclaimed by the angel as good news from the Greek word, *"euangelizo."* Within the contexts of these gospel passages is the quaking response of condemned sinners before the presence of the glorious light of Christ.

In Exodus 24:16-17, Acts 26:12-14, and the account of the shepherds in Luke 2:9, the illuminating glory of the Lord causes the onlookers to tremble because his light reveals that they are helplessly unresponsive, perpetually hopeless, and unregenerate and unaware.

Helplessly Unresponsive

Jesus actually summarized his parabolic ministry by looking back to Isaiah's commission and showing the same focus. The Son of God saw himself as picking up where Isaiah had left off:

Matt. 13:13–17 *This is why I speak to them in parables, because seeing they do not see, and hearing they do not hear, nor do they understand. Indeed, in their case the prophecy of Isaiah is fulfilled that says:*
"You will indeed hear but never understand,
and you will indeed see but never perceive.

---

[15] David E. Garland, *Luke*, Zondervan Exegetical Commentary on the New Testament (Grand Rapids: Zondervan, 2011), 122.

For this people's heart has grown dull,
and with their ears they can barely hear,
and their eyes they have closed,
lest they should see with their eyes
and hear with their ear
and understand with their heart and turn,
and I would heal them."
But blessed are your eyes, for they see, and your ears, for they hear. For truly, I say to you, many prophets and righteous people longed to see what you see, and did not see it, and to hear what you hear, and did not hear it.

This could seem confusing. Why would people understand the basic point or moral of a parable and yet still not believe in Jesus? Jesus's parables were not obscure. Unbelievers approach parables in a way similar to reading well-known fables, while the illumined person moves beyond the superficial clarity of parables to the actual meaning and deeper implications. Jonathan Edwards, the notable 18th-century preacher, helps to clarify this:

> It is possible that a man might know how to interpret all the types, parables, enigmas, and allegories in the Bible, and not have one beam of spiritual light in his mind; because he may not have the least degree of that spiritual sense of the holy beauty of divine things which has been spoken of, and may see nothing of this kind of glory in anything contained in any of these mysteries, or any other part of the Scripture.[16]

Edwards is saying that illumination—knowing the Lord's "holy beauty"—is distinct from simple interpretation. This is an important distinction to make when thinking about what Jesus really meant about "seeing" and "hearing" truth. As stated at the beginning of this work, whether or not a person is illumined is truly a matter of spiritual life and death. The unillumined—that is to say unbelievers—may be in the position of professors at seminaries, Bible Colleges, in the pulpit, or may even be the world's leading exegetical author or influential spiritual leader. None of these positions or accomplishments qualify a person as illumined. Any of these people may be an unforgiven sinner still guilty before the LORD and condemned for their sins. It is sad when this is the case, but history has shown that many who did not have "ears to hear" or "eyes to see" have entered ministry to the determent of the people they have led. We have seen how the ministry of Hophni and Phineas was marked by condemnation and further drove the people into

---

[16] Jonathan Edwards, *The Religious Affections* (Carlisle, PA: Banner of Truth, 1746; 1986), 204.

further condemnation and blindness. This next example shows how a condemned person remains blind to effectual power of Scripture even in death. The only cure for blindness is sight, and this sight comes only from the power of God the Holy Spirit and the proclaimed Word (Jas. 1:18; 1 Pet. 1:22–23).

Perpetual Hopelessness

Perhaps one of the saddest examples of a condemned person rejecting the efficacy of Scripture is the story the Lord told in Luke 16:19–31. This is the account of the rich man and Lazarus, which many understand to be a parable. This story reads like one of Jesus's parables, but Jesus uses real names, which seems to indicate real people in a real historical setting. Jesus never used names in any of his other parables. Either way, this is perhaps one of the most sobering stories in the Bible. Jesus told of two men:

Luke 16:19–31 *There was a rich man who was clothed in purple and fine linen and who feasted sumptuously every day. And at his gate was laid a poor man named Lazarus, covered with sores, who desired to be fed with what fell from the rich man's table. Moreover, even the dogs came and licked his sores. The poor man died and was carried by the angels to Abraham's side. The rich man also died and was buried, and in Hades, being in torment, he lifted up his eyes and saw Abraham far off and Lazarus at his side. And he called out, "Father Abraham, have mercy on me, and send Lazarus to dip the end of his finger in water and cool my tongue, for I am in anguish in this flame." But Abraham said, "Child, remember that you in your lifetime received your good things, and Lazarus in like manner bad things; but now he is comforted here, and you are in anguish. And besides all this, between us and you a great chasm has been fixed, in order that those who would pass from here to you may not be able, and none may cross from there to us." And he said, "Then I beg you, father, to send him to my father's house—for I have five brothers—so that he may warn them, lest they also come into this place of torment." But Abraham said, "They have Moses and the Prophets; let them hear them." And he said, "No, father Abraham, but if someone goes to them from the dead, they will repent." He said to him, "If they do not hear Moses and the Prophets, neither will they be convinced if someone should rise from the dead."*

Much could be said about this passage, but note how the rich man begs that Lazarus be sent back to warn his five brothers, keeping them from suffering eternal hell as he is (vv. 27–28). The Lord's response is amazing. Abraham, understood here to be the Lord, says, "They have Moses and the Prophets; let them hear them" (v. 29). The Lord is not so much rebuking the rich man as affirming the transforming power of the Word of God. The rich man, missing the point, makes the case that, though his brothers might ignore the Word, they would surely repent if they encountered a miraculous resurrected messenger sent specifically to them (v. 30). Abraham's final statement to the rich man reveals the true nature of what it means to be under this condemnation. He says, "If they do not hear Moses and the Prophets, neither will they be convinced if someone should rise from the dead" (v. 31). No amount of sensationalism will change a heart that is rejecting the light. A person who will not see spiritual light from the Word will not see God's glorious light displayed in miracles.

Unregenerate and Unaware

Jesus's words in John's Gospel further confirm this sobering reality. For most Christians, John 3:16 is the quintessential call to believe and receive eternal life, but people often forget what Jesus said in verse 18. Though Jesus guaranteed eternal life for all who believe, he also stated what is equally true—those who do not believe are "condemned already." They are presently in a state of condemnation, which may end up as eternal condemnation without the Lord. Jesus described people in this state as those who reject light because light exposes their moral darkness (vv. 19–20). This is the sad plight for people presently condemned—they want their sin, which is killing and damning them, yet they need Jesus's rescue.

Those who reject the powerful and transforming message of God's Word are in the same state as so many eyewitnesses of Jesus's miracles. They remained cynical, not willing to fully embrace Jesus as God. Jesus performed miracles to reveal himself as God, but he was not naïve regarding the fickle nature of most who followed him. Scripture documents Jesus's response, stating that he "did not entrust himself to them, because he knew all people" (John 2:24). They did not give themselves to Jesus, and Jesus did not give himself to them. The crowds were not illumined, but condemned.

Claiming to follow Jesus while being condemned is indicative of having a false sense of illumination. Their illumination is not founded upon the light of Christ, but on a light emanating from the world, a light that skews the biblical teaching of condemnation or completely rejects it. This so-called light is a false illumination.

FALSE ILLUMINATION

Believing in a gospel that is void of condemnation is the deadliest situation for a person to find himself in. Mankind's natural response to the message of condemnation is to invalidate its truth. To them, it is nonsensical that all people are blind sinners and have no ability in and of themselves to be awakened to truth. Either of these rejections are deadly. A person has no means to see the light of the gospel. He is utterly incapable.

Let me explain the seriousness of removing the teaching of condemnation from the gospel. Rejecting condemnation is to preach a gospel that starts with an illumination that originates within oneself. During the Enlightenment, condemnation was widely rejected and replaced with a "self-defining" gospel.

Such worldly ideologies appear to have a brilliance similar to that of the gospel and even claim to fall under the banner of "gospel truth." When these man-centric movements are compared with Scripture, they are found wanting of true illumination. They are an example of a pseudo-illumination. Since Scripture abundantly and clearly presents the doctrine of illumination, evangelicalism contains a broad interpretation of this teaching. Such a reality is recipe for disaster.

Look at the book of Hebrews, an epistle filled with warnings. Here is written what is perhaps the most frightening and sobering condemnation of gospel-rejecters in the entire Bible: "For it is impossible, in the case of those who have once been enlightened, who have tasted the heavenly gift, and have shared in the Holy Spirit, and have tasted the goodness of the word of God and the powers of the age to come, and then have fallen away, to restore them again to repentance" (6:4–6). Out of all the passages on spiritual blindness in the New Testament, this is probably the most stinging, and also the most applicable to today's church. These verses rebuke anybody who would dare to play church or fake Christianity. In other words, true biblical illumination can't be forged. A pseudo-illuminated Christianity distorts an accurate teaching of illumination.

This section in Hebrews describes self-professed believers who have experienced superficial repentance and have been enlightened in a merely external sense. These superficial experiences have come from tasting spiritual realities—the "believers" have been enjoying the benefits of God that come to his people and have been seeing his power all around them. They have been exposed to answered prayers, powerful preaching, powerful worship, counsel, sacrificial love, and much more, all while never really letting go of their love for sin and never really giving themselves to Jesus. They have just enough light from the Holy Spirit to experience God's power, yet they still turn their backs on the truth of the gospel, spurning Jesus Christ. The Bible is here warning that rejecting Christ after being exposed at this level to God's revelation renders people beyond reach—they are condemned.

Resolved to Preach Condemnation

This kind of talk does not stop with Jesus. The book of Acts also speaks of condemnation in the account of Stephen, a man known by the early church to be "full faith and of the Holy Spirit" (6:5). Stephen's tenacity was sure to cause friction with unbelievers. From the record in Acts, it seems that very soon after he was affirmed for church leadership, he was falsely accused of being a troublemaker by those in the synagogue with whom he "disputed." He found himself having to testify before a hostile tribunal with his life on the line (6:9–7:1). Stephen's sermon pulled no punches. He ended up condemning his hearers as deaf men, much as Isaiah and Jesus did.

Unrelenting Preaching

Scripture's teaching of condemnation does not pull any punches, so neither did Stephen in his proclamation of this truth. His descriptions were meant to sting. He said, "You stiff-necked people, uncircumcised in heart and ears, you always resist the Holy Spirit. As your fathers did, so do you" (Acts 7:51). His audience did not appreciate his assessment of them. Their angry response makes this obvious: "But they cried out with a loud voice and stopped their ears and rushed together at him" (v. 57). Luke, the descriptive and detailed author of Acts, points out that they plugged their ears—a physical expression of outright rejection of the truth. This hardness of heart turned murderous—they attacked and killed Stephen (v. 58). It does not take long for persecution against those who hold fast to the gospel to manifest. In the first edition of *Illuminated Preaching* printed in 2010, I wrote that "Persecution of this kind is very foreign to Western believers today." Many churches are violently opposed to the message that genuine belief in Jesus is the only way to heaven, that their own sin has offended a holy God, and that unless they repent of it, they will suffer a deserved punishment in hell forever.

Throughout the book of Acts, the early church grew by leaps and bounds by means of gospel preaching. This same preaching was part of the ministry of condemnation. Paul's summary of his ministry, which serves as a postscript to Acts, contains a direct reference to Isaiah 6 and places Paul's ministry in the same preaching lineage. First Isaiah, then Jesus, then Stephen, and now Paul were all rejected by God's chosen people. Quoting Isaiah 6:9, Paul put himself right in this stream of rejection, saying,

Acts 28:25–27 *The Holy Spirit was right in saying to your fathers through Isaiah the prophet:*
"Go to this people, and say,
    'You will indeed hear but never understand,

and you will indeed see but never perceive.
 For this people's heart has grown dull,
and with their ears they can barely hear,
 and their eyes they have closed;
lest they should see with their eyes
 and hear with their ears
and understand with their heart and turn,
 and I would heal them.'"

Isaiah, Paul, Stephen and our Lord Jesus Christ were rejected and martyred for an unrelenting commitment to preach the essential doctrine that all of mankind is utterly blind without the illuminating light of Christ.

Uncompromised Preaching

Paul went on to expand this theme in his New Testament epistles. In his letter to the Romans, he referred to the Jews' present blind state, saying, "God gave them a spirit of stupor, eyes that would not see and ears that would not hear, down to this very day" (11:8). Paul did not stop with the Jews, but also exhorted one of his most beloved New Testament churches along these same lines.

In 2 Thessalonians, Paul warned the church not to fall into deception regarding the timing of the Day of the Lord. He specifically marked the end times by the coming of "the man of lawlessness," who is the Anti-Christ (2 Thess. 2:3). Paul wrote that many in the end would be deceived by this man and characterized that man's leadership as "the activity of Satan" (v. 9). Just as in 2 Corinthians 4:1–4, Satan is here seen as the agent of deception. Paul spoke of people as being in a state of "perishing" because of their sin and refusing "to love the truth" (v. 10). They are then ultimately "condemned" (v. 12): "Therefore God sends them a strong delusion, so that they may believe what is false, in order that all may be condemned who did not believe the truth but had pleasure in unrighteousness."

In Ephesians, Paul condemned Gentile blindness, saying that the Gentiles "… are darkened in their understanding … due to their hardness of heart" (Eph. 4:18). He then picked on the false teachers in the church, pointing out that they were "… never able to arrive at a knowledge of the truth" (2 Tim. 3:7). Paul had the same result from preaching that Jesus did. For some, his ministry was a savor of life to life, but for others, it was death to death (2 Cor. 2:16).

Our Need to Preach Condemnation

This chapter has shown that, at the core, people are spiritually blind and deaf to God's Word because of sin. Sin acts as a fog, clouding man's ability to perceive the gospel's glory and truthfulness and turning a person's heart away from God toward Satan's kingdom and the things of the world. Satan operates in tandem with man's own sin, covering the eyes of unbelievers to keep them from seeing Jesus's shining face (2 Cor. 4:4). The disconnect between unbelievers and truth is not on a cognitive level.

Instead, as one homiletics scholar put it, the truth simply comes across "to their unregenerate judgment [as] … 'foolishness' or nonsense to their unredeemed minds."[17] He continues, "Facts inform but only the Spirit transforms, and that is what is missing when the Spirit's illumination is not present."[18] The Bible offers hope, for although this first stage of illumination can be rejected, it can also serve as what Owen called "preparatory operations on the souls of men."[19] Under this first stage, Owen admitted, "Many are thus enlightened, and yet never converted," but this light can be "in order of nature … previous to conversion, and … materially preparatory to [conversion] … for saving grace enters into the soul by light … therefore, a gift of God."[20] He knew that "… the word preached is the instrumental cause" for genuine conversion to take place.[21]

Understanding what God's Word says about the condemnation that occurs because of gospel proclamation is important in shaping the Christian's expectations of understanding Scripture for himself. For the preacher, this has significant implications for his preaching. These implications are also significant for teachers in the church, evangelists, and the faithful woman teaching younger women God's Word and how to love their husbands.

These servants do not really know God's goals when they communicate truth, since God's will regarding each and every ministry is secret (see Deut. 29:29). It may seem that God is using his Word as a tool to judge condemned sinners more often than to convert them. This concept can be discouraging. It might cause a heart to feel defeated and say, "Why even bother to study God's Word? Why preach or proclaim condemnation when most of the people who hear me will never change?"

---

[17] Greg Heisler, *Spirit-Led Preaching: The Holy Spirit's Role in Sermon Preparation and Delivery* (Nashville: B & H Academic, 2007), 46.
[18] Ibid.
[19] John Owen, *The Holy Spirit: His Gifts and Power* (Grand Rapids: Kregel, 1954), 135.
[20] Ibid., 38.
[21] Ibid., 137.

Instead of thinking that, think about this: the pressure actually disappears with the realization that life-change for the hearer is not won and lost by the preacher's or evangelist's performance. How well he communicates is not the determining factor as to whether or not people spiritually grasp truth. This does not mean there is a free pass to become a lazy Bible student or sloppy communicator. On the contrary, knowing that illumination is God's work frees the Christian to focus on communicating God's Word with clarity, as opposed to focusing on style or relevance. It assures the faithful disciple of Jesus Christ to proclaim the gospel from the clarity of Scripture rather than from the demands of a changing culture.

Practically, this leads to great freedom in ministry, since the Christian's heart is focused on being faithful, handling the truth with integrity, and trusting God with the results—regardless of whether God chooses to convict or condemn, bring spiritual life or death, wound or heal. Regardless of the result, the Lord gets glory (2 Cor. 2:15–16).

Paul's firm grasp on this concept made him unflappable in his preaching ministry, and he was able to say "we do not lose heart" (2 Cor. 4:1). He stayed the course and did not become a manipulator of people's emotions but remained a faithful communicator of truth, leaving the results to God (v. 2). Calvin's persevering and powerful testimony also came from understanding this. He well understood both the source of spiritual blindness and its remedy, illumination. He documented this, saying,

> Our mind is too rude to be able to comprehend the spiritual wisdom of God which is revealed to us by faith, and our hearts are too prone either to diffidence or to a perverse confidence in ourselves or creatures, to rest in God of their own accord. But the Holy Spirit by his illumination makes us capable of understanding those things which would otherwise far exceed our capacity, and forms us to a firm persuasion, by sealing the promises of salvation on our hearts.[22]

It is a sobering reality that people are condemned by their sin; however, God's Word provides the remedy. The Lord has provided the means for the lights to be turned on—simply by allowing people to hear the truth. From the very beginning, God has illumined communicators of his Word so that they will preach, and hearers will be illumined.

---

[22] John Calvin, Henry Beveridge, tr., *Tracts and Treatises on the Doctrine and Worship of the Church* (Grand Rapids: Eerdmans, 1849; 1958), 2:53.

5

Communication for Illumination

2 Cor. 4:5 *For what we proclaim is not ourselves, but Jesus Christ as Lord, with ourselves as your servants for Jesus' sake.*

How is God's Word meant to bring about change? Think about this: the most monumental physical change that ever took place began with God speaking—he spoke creation into existence. God said, "'Let there be light,' and there was light" (Gen. 1:3). These simple words from God are the genesis of everything anyone who has ever lived has ever seen or felt. Likewise, God's revealed Word brings about monumental spiritual change. His Word transforms lives blinded by Satan and lost in sin, changing them into believers who love the glory of Christ Jesus.

The doctrine of the Bible teaches two fundamental principles for approaching Scripture. Of first importance is the character of Scripture. We learn from 1 Timothy 3:16 that every word of Scripture is inspired, "θεόπνευστος," which literally means "God-breathed." Scripture has its origin from God himself. This means the characteristics of Scripture are the characteristics of God. John MacArthur explains this relationship well, "In Scripture, the person of God and the Word of God are everywhere interrelated, so much so that whatever is true about the character of God is true about the nature of God's Word."[23] One bedrock truth that comes from this teaching is that since God is authoritative and completely sufficient, so is his Word. When it comes to preaching God's Word, calling people to trust in God's Word is the evidence that the preacher in fact believes in Scripture's suffi-

---

[23] MacArthur and Mayhue, *Biblical Doctrine*, 70.

ciency. A danger looms in the preaching task. While God's Word is completely and perfectly sufficient, its message will be compromised when it is intertwined with the insufficiency of fallen humanity. Therefore, the preacher must be diligent to know that the message he preaches is not his own message, rather, it is about Christ (2 Cor. 4:5). The preacher must ask, "whose words am I preaching?"

WHOSE WORDS?

Perhaps one of the most fundamental validations that the Lord works through his Word is that the New Testament demands that qualified men preach the Word to effect change (2 Tim. 4:1–2). Though preaching is still being carried out in various forms and fashions in the church today, there are new preaching philosophies and methods that ignore and undermine its biblically defined purpose. These man-centered philosophies demand the preacher to disregard the reliability and authority of Scripture.

Instead of having a disposition that sets aside the reliability and authority of Scripture, the faithful preacher commits himself to preaching the Word according to a method that is founded on a high view of God. How do we know that our preaching promotes a high view of God?

A High View of God's Word Means a Low View of Man's Word

Scripture clearly and authoritatively affirms the essential doctrine of God's Word as the only message that can bring about such a heart transformation. God repeatedly warns against the words of the self-proclaimed wise men of this age (Prov. 3:5-7; 26:5, 12; 28:11). Solomon, in all his wisdom warned against the temptation of becoming arrogant and trusting one's own ability to do good and to understand (Eccl. 7:16). Where is evangelicalism today and how does it compare with God's standard for communication. What is God's standard for preaching?

Authority of Scripture

Biblical proclamation of the Word declares the truth that stands on the unmovable pillars of God's indiscriminate Word. The preacher proclaims the truth to all and for all. He first preaches the Word to himself because he has the utmost regard for the Word and believes every Word to be inspired, infallible, perspicuous, inerrant, sufficient, preserved, and authoritative. His mind has been illumined to the words that are before his eyes. He is compelled to announce this truth as if he were yielding a golden trumpet. He does not hide the trumpet; he does not discard it for a trumpet made of bronze or metal. No, he proclaims the sounds clearly and accurately for all to hear. When the preacher inserts his opinion into the sermon, it loses all authority. When the preacher proclaims the very words of God, the message is authoritative. Those who disregard the authority of the message are destined to reject the Word itself.

Perspicuity of Scripture

The relationship of the perspicuity of Scripture to the illumination of the Holy Spirit is that when the preacher has done his job in studying the text to ascertain God's original meaning of the text by a grammatical, literal, and historical study, he can be confident that his preaching is communicating God's clear message so long as his preaching is communicating exactly what is in God's Word. This is the heart of expositional preaching; therefore, any preaching that is not expositional does not belong in churches.

Unbelievers reject Christ because he is light. Only those who have been illuminated by the one who illumines accept Christ for who he is: God.

John 3:20–21 *For everyone who does wicked things hates the light and does not come to the light, lest his works should be exposed. But whoever does what is true comes to the light, so that it may be clearly seen that his works have been carried out in God.*

Unbelievers are blinded to the gospel (2 Cor. 4:4) and are helplessly unable to welcome its truth because they don't possess the ability to even see it. A biblical theology of illumination is, therefore, inseparably connected to the doctrine of the perspicuity of Scripture.

Sufficiency of Scripture

That God's Word is authoritative and clear demands preachers to communicate to the hearers that they must obey his Word. This is foundational to preaching. Another elementary but forgotten teaching and practice is that God's Word is completely sufficient. Scripture is as sufficient as God is sufficient. But what about man's word? We have different experiences that shape our ideas and thoughts that can impact the methods used in ministry. What does God's Word say about the reliability of man's word in the context of preaching?

GRASS, FLOWERS, AND GOD'S WORD

Isaiah was a preacher of preachers among the Old Testament prophets. The theme of a high view of God permeates his prophetic book (cf. 2:11;

40:3; 66:1–3; etc.). The preacher especially notes a certain implication that goes along with a high view of God's Word in Isaiah 40:6–8, namely, a low view of man and his word.

Is. 40:6–8 *A voice says, "Cry!" And I said, "What shall I cry?" All flesh is grass, and all its beauty is like the flower of the field. The grass withers, the flower fades when the breath of the Lord blows on it; surely the people are grass. The grass withers, the flower fades, but the word of our God will stand forever.*

This declaration of the sufficiency of God's Word is pronounced within the context of Isaiah giving Israel encouragement and explaining to them that Yahweh their God will one day deliver them from bondage. Isaiah then calls this announcement the good news (v. 9)! So, what we are about to read was given in the very context of God's ability to save his people. Isaiah is preaching a message of salvation.

A voice says, "Cry!" And I said, "What shall I cry?"

It doesn't take thirty hours of study to understand the urgency God is calling for in these verses. To properly display the urgency and emphasis of the message to follow these instructions to "cry" or "proclaim," you would need a megaphone. Now, before we dig into the meat of these verses, we must remember the major point of these verses, which is the quality of God's Word: "but the Word of the LORD endures forever." This occurs as the last statement of this urgent cry God has given to the prophet. Everything in these verses informs us of the nature of God's Word.

All flesh is grass, and all its beauty is like the flower of the field. The grass withers, the flower fades when the breath of the Lord blows on it; surely the people are grass.

Framing the declaration of the supreme sufficiency of Scripture are two descriptions of the insufficiency of the nature of mankind. The prophet first compares humanity to grass. It's significant to note that Isaiah isn't speaking for his own ethnic group or culture alone. This truth is bound to the fabric of the fallen condition of all humanity. Who is grass? Everyone. What is grass? Here, grass is defined by what it does: it dies easily. Can we rely on grass to accomplish a lot? No. Are we able to accomplish a lot? I think we get the idea. Grass doesn't last long, and neither do we, because we have something called human nature. Now, most of us are keenly aware of the truth behind Isaiah's first botanical illustration, but Isaiah doesn't stop his gardening project.

Isaiah's second illustration paints a more specific quality of human nature that is insufficient. Many translations, such as the ESV, read "all its beauty is like the flower of the field." At first, we might have the picture of a person's outward beauty fading as he or she advances in years. While poetic, this is not the picture the original hearers of Isaiah's message would have had in mind. The word translated as "beauty" is the Hebrew word "*hesed*." Throughout the Old Testament, *hesed* is used in reference to Yahweh's unfailing trustworthy commitment to his people based on his covenantal promise. In these verses, the quality of man's *hesed* is in question. While the Word of Yahweh endures forever, man's *hesed*, or trustworthiness, is as reliable as a flower that withers in the wind.

The grass withers, the flower fades, but the word of our God will stand forever.

Isaiah now contrasts the insufficiency of man's words to the sufficiency of God's Word. Grass represents the limitedness of human nature. Flowers represent the untrustworthiness of human nature. So, Isaiah puts his megaphone up to his mouth, takes a deep breath, and shouts "all people are limited, and all people are untrustworthy, but God's Word is eternally trustworthy!"

As Christians, we must be on guard against attempts to interject the nature of man into God's Word. One common attempt is to integrate psychological methods such as behavior modification, cognitive brain therapy, and psychotropic medication with God's Word. Is God's Word sufficient for our spiritual life, or does the Word need modification? Another example of where man's "wisdom" is encroaching into American churches is the attempt to harmonize people's stories with the story of God's Word to understand the Bible more accurately. It's one thing to use our stories of God working in our lives to build relationships and get to know one another; however, the "story" approach necessitates one's life story as a prerequisite to understand God. Isaiah is screaming out to us that there is no room for our words or thoughts to intermix with the Word of the Holy One of Israel. Our sinful nature and insufficiency will inevitably distort and disrupt the holy and pure nature of God's Word.

Rejecting a High View of Scripture

While these truths clearly permeate Scripture, the culture that we live in has been attempting to persuade pastors, biblical counselors, and missionaries to utilize man-centered philosophies when it comes to communicating the gospel.

God's prescribed communication method is non-negotiable. Rejecting God's communication reveals a heart that is not transformed by God's Word. Evangelicalism has been abandoning God's mandated standards of preaching and enlisting themselves under the doctrine of a man-centric philosophy of communication. Choosing man's communication over God's has one inevitable end: "Be not overly righteous, and do not make yourself too wise. Why should you destroy yourself?" (Eccl. 7:16).

6
Illumined Communicators

The Bible emphasizes not only illumined communication but also illumined communicators. In the earliest biblical record, God is seen strategically speaking to patriarchs such as Noah, Abraham, Isaac, Jacob, Joseph, and Moses. When these men heard the LORD's communication, they became God's spokesmen. Old and New Testament prophets received direct revelation from God. This differs from preachers, who communicate from the revelation that has already been given. However, there remains significant overlap in how the Holy Spirit illumines the minds of both prophets and preachers on the basis of revelation.

OLD PREACHERS: THE SAME SPIRIT

Genesis is properly called "the book of beginnings," for God reveals many of his beginning works in the book. From Adam to Abraham to Jacob, Genesis reveals God's beginning work of creation, redemption, and the election of a chosen people. At the climax of the book (chapters 37-50), God calls Joseph to be his mouthpiece to proclaim his will. God's interaction with Joseph gives a clear example of how God turned men into his mouthpieces.

Joseph as God's Communicator

As the story goes, Joseph had been imprisoned by Pharaoh due to false accusations, and then through a series of God-planned circumstances, he was recommended by Pharaoh's chief cupbearer to interpret a symbolic dream

(Gen. 39–41). Because none of Pharaoh's magicians or wise men could interpret the dream and Joseph could, Pharaoh said, "Can we find a man like this, in whom is the Spirit of God?" Then Pharaoh said to Joseph, "Since God has shown you all this, there is none so discerning and wise as you are" (41:38–39). The implication from the text is that Joseph was spiritually illumined to communicate God's will to Pharaoh. It is illumination that produces the very things for which Joseph was commended: discernment and wisdom.

Moses the Prophet–Preacher

Moses was an illuminated prophet who brought God's message to God's people. Milestone accomplishments through his life have brought attention to his character as God's foremost illuminated communicator. When it comes to being God's illuminated communicator, Moses is most popularly known for his role in the communication of God's Law to his people. Moses is the human author of the first five books of the Old Testament, Genesis through Deuteronomy. Additionally, his experience in receiving the Law from the LORD on the mountain top of Sinai, in which he saw God, was uniquely illuminating. Moses came down from the mountain top illumined, and his encounter with the Holy God who is light reflected in his appearance being changed. Among mere men, Moses was truly the illumined prophet of his day.

Judges: No Preachers in Those Days

In the book of Judges, a serious lack of spiritual leadership loomed over the land, casting a dark shroud of spiritual blindness over it. How did the light of God's Word get hidden under a basket? Retracing the lack of preachers committed to the proclamation of the Word in the days of the judges demonstrates one of the factors that led to Israel's darkest days of despondency (3:1).

Judges begins with the passing of leadership from Joshua to the tribe of Judah. The newly appointed leading tribe is marked by passionately conquering the territory allotted to them, while the other tribes neglect their responsibility or intermix with the inhabiting Canaanites. The tribe of Judah imprints a picture of a people who not only knew God's Word but also passionately applied it to their lives. It would seem as if Moses' and Joshua's preaching career left a positive impression on the tribe of Judah. However, not all of the tribes harkened to the words of the patriarchs. Consequently, they utterly failed in completing the conquest, resulting in the Caananization of the land and the beginning of what Daniel Block describes as "the downward spiral of Israelite faith and conduct."[24]

As preachers of God's Word in the midst of a crooked and twisted generation (Phil. 2:15), we must not let our pulpit be defined by the culture. Since we are in a position to proclaim messages to people, culture demands us to use this venue to preach prosperity, wealth and health, social justice, political activity, and other temporal agendas which have no eternal value. These threats to the purity of the Word are not always easily detectible. Many who claim a "Christ-centered" pulpit subtly surround their messages with manmade agendas and ideologies.

Christ must not only be central in the pulpit, but he must also be preeminent throughout the preaching with no competition. He shares his glory with no other (Is. 42:8). The truth of Christ's light must be proclaimed to every corner of the house so as to not give any room for darkness to hide. Social agendas in the pulpit attempts to share glory with Christ and this practice must be quenched. History never runs short of usurpers, rioters, looters, corrupt political leaders, and the like. Preachers must not attempt to feed a leviathan that will never be satisfied. Preachers must never compromise from feeding their sheep the whole counsel of God. Such a task satisfies the preacher's call and the believer's soul.

Kings: Leaders Dawn Out of Darkness

After the time of the patriarchs and the judges, God raised up kings to lead his people. These men possessed the massive responsibilities of reading God's Word to the people that God had entrusted to them. This entrustment included the responsibility to rule their people, a task which carried with them the expectation that the kings would possess spiritual discernment. What is notable is the means by which the kings were instructed to acquire this. The book of the Law required them to carefully read the Law, God's Word, and then to write a word-for-word copy of it.

Leadership and God's Word

This command can be found in the book of Deuteronomy: "And when he sits on the throne of his kingdom, he shall write for himself in a book a copy of this law, approved by the Levitical priests" (17:18). The king needed to "read in it all the days of his life," with the result that he would "learn to

---

[24] Daniel I. Block, *Judges, Ruth*, vol. 6, New American Commentary (Nashville: B & H Publishers, 1999), 131.

fear the LORD his God by keeping all the words of this law and these statutes and doing them" (v. 19). This exercise gave recognition to the fact that, in a very real sense, this revelation was just as authentic and powerful for each succeeding generation as when the Pentateuch was first written. For the king, it would be almost as if God were speaking audibly to him. Though spiritual illumination is not directly mentioned, the clear implication is that the king's fear of the LORD would come from spiritual illumination (see 2 Sam. 23:1–3; Prov. 1:7; Is. 11:2–4; Mic. 6:9; Acts 13:26; 2 Cor. 7:1; Heb. 4:1).

Don't miss the serious connection between the king and the Scripture. The king was entrusted with the weighty responsibility of ruling over the LORD's nation. Throughout his lifetime he would make significant decisions with regard to the physical and spiritual well-being of his people. What was the prescribed key to success? He needed to be illumined by God's Law to fear the LORD.

David's Role as Anointed King

Spiritual illumination was essential in order for the king to reign with success over Israel. Look at what the prophet Samuel said to Israel's first king, Saul. Samuel prophesied, saying, "… the Spirit of the LORD will rush upon you, and you will prophesy with them and be turned into another man" (1 Sam. 10:6). Because of Saul's wicked character, his illumination was superficial and temporary. He ultimately turned away from God; yet as king, he possessed the ability to prophesy and communicate for God for a time. In the early days, spiritual communication marked Saul's rule (1 Sam. 19:24), but his character eventually caused him to lose his kingship.

Saul's successor was David, a man with godly character who was illumined to communicate God's truth to the end of his life. In 2 Samuel, there is a significant epitaph regarding David's life and ministry that testifies to this:

2 Sam. 23:1–3 *Now these are the last words of David: The oracle of David, the son of Jesse, the oracle of the man who was raised on high, the anointed of the God of Jacob, the sweet psalmist of Israel: "The Spirit of the LORD speaks by me; his word is on my tongue. The God of Israel has spoken; the Rock of Israel has said to me: When one rules justly over men, ruling in the fear of God …"*

No other time in David's life better demonstrates David's passion for spiritual illumination than when he thought he had lost it. He knew that possessing this gift from God was a high privilege and essential for him as king of Israel. When he was immoral with Bathsheba and followed that with a massive cover-up scandal (2 Sam. 11:2–21), he knew he was in serious danger of having his gift stripped away by the LORD.

He eventually repented of his sin, and what stands out here is the significant emphasis he placed on begging the LORD that he might not lose spiritual illumination. He prayed, "Cast me not away from your presence, and take not your Holy Spirit from me" (Ps. 51:11). By asking that God would not take the Holy Spirit from him, he was not trying to protect his eternal salvation; this was not David's struggle. Rather, he was asking God that he be allowed to maintain a rule empowered by the Spirit, even though he had committed adultery and orchestrated Uriah's murder—acts that were both punishable by death. Amazingly, God honored this request by not only granting him forgiveness but also allowing David to continue as king. Psalm 32 attests to this.

Though he was simply a frail human being, King David foreshadowed the Messiah, the one who was to come, the ultimate King, and the one who came as the ultimate Spirit-anointed communicator. The prophet Isaiah characterized Christ and his ministry as illumined by the Spirit when he said:

Is. 11:1–2 *There shall come forth a shoot from the stump of Jesse,*
  and a branch from his roots shall bear fruit.
And the Spirit of the LORD shall rest upon him,
  Spirit of wisdom and understanding,
the Spirit of counsel and might,
  the Spirit of knowledge and the fear of the LORD.

It is fitting that David's son Solomon, next in line to the throne, prayed for this same spiritual discernment.

1 Kings 3:9 *Give your servant therefore an understanding mind to govern your people, that I may discern between good and evil, for who is able to govern this your great people?"*

God honored his wise request as he did with David, and 1 Kings 4:29 documents this, saying, "… God gave Solomon wisdom and understanding beyond measure, and breadth of mind like the sand on the seashore." Solomon had the reputation among the nations in his day of being the wisest man who had ever lived. It is only fitting that he authored the majority of the Bible's wisdom literature—the Song of Solomon, much of Proverbs, as well as the book of Ecclesiastes, which is, in effect, a twelve-chapter sermon delivered by "the Preacher," the "the son of David" (Eccl. 1:1).

Judges Take Two: The Failure of Leadership

As the dark days of the judges demonstrated, when there is a lack of men of God who will proclaim God's Word, there will be a want of spiritual appetite for the Lord. David demonstrated such a trend with his sin with Bathsheba. When he was supposed to be out leading his men in war, he disrobed his leadership and committed adultery. David's sin is not far off from pastors today who neglect shepherding the sheep that the Lord has entrusted to them and instead adulterate themselves with alluring philosophies and captivating trends of the culture that taints the pure gospel. David's sin became paradigmatic in the life of the next king of Israel. David's son Solomon would disobey God's strict and direct commands for leaders. God commanded the kings of Israel that they were not to multiply horses, gold, nor wives for themselves (Deut. 17:16–17). Solomon did all three. His leadership ministry was tainted. His ability to lead God's people was marred by his direct disobedience to God's Word.

Preacher's today must maintain a life of integrity, holiness, and blamelessness. There is no standard higher than what is set for the preacher of God's Word. The stakes are too high. God has the preacher in a critical position of leadership in Christ's church. He has illumined the pastor to preach the Word. If darkness is seen in the pastor's life, it could be construed that such darkness emanates from God's Word. Such was the case for the era of the book of Kings. After Solomon, king after king continually did what was evil in the sight of the LORD. God's Word was severely neglected during this era. Such is indicated at the close of the era of the kings when Josiah discovers the book of the Law. He discovers the Pentateuch written by Moses, reads it, and weeps. It would have been similar to the moment that Martin Luther was struck by the Spirit with the truth that the just shall live by faith. Josiah's discovery of God's Word was followed by reform. Whenever God's Word is recovered, there is reformation.

A NEW DAWN OF PREACHERS

The Gospels confirm that Isaiah's prophecy came true. Jesus came and bannered his entire earthly ministry by quoting Isaiah 61:1 (see Luke 4:18). In the synagogue, he read Isaiah with reference to himself, which says,

Is. 61:1 *The Spirit of the Lord GOD is upon me,*
because the LORD has anointed me to bring good news to the poor;
he has sent me to bind up the brokenhearted,
to proclaim liberty to the captives,
and the opening of the prison to those who are bound ...

Because Jesus is God, it might seem that Jesus did not need the Holy Spirit when he preached. However, he still made the clear connection between the Holy Spirit's anointing and his role as a gospel communicator. Though Jesus, as both God and man, was the quintessential communicator, he came in the tradition of the rest of the prophets—Jeremiah, Ezekiel, Daniel, and all the others anointed to speak for God. We know that the Lord Jesus knew preaching to be his mandate, not only because he characterized his ministry under the banner of Isaiah 61:1, but also because of the statement he made just on the heels of this, when he said, "I must preach the good news of the kingdom of God to the other towns as well; for I was sent for this purpose" (Luke 4:43). Jesus fulfilled this preaching ministry, and those who followed in his steps likewise became examples of illumined communicators.

Spirit-Anointed Preachers

Luke told in his Gospel of the godly man Simeon who spent his life waiting in the temple for Jesus the Messiah to be born. In his account of Simeon's experience when Christ was first presented at the temple, Luke emphasized the dawning of the new spiritual day. He wrote,

Luke 2:25–32 *Now there was a man in Jerusalem, whose name was Simeon, and this man was righteous and devout, waiting for the consolation of Israel, and the Holy Spirit was upon him. And it had been revealed to him by the Holy Spirit that he would not see death before he had seen the Lord's Christ. And he came in the Spirit into the temple, and when the parents brought in the child Jesus, to do for him according to the custom of the Law, he took him up in his arms and blessed God and said, "Lord, now you are letting your servant depart in peace, according to your word; for my eyes have seen your salvation that you have prepared in the presence of all peoples, a light for revelation to the Gentiles, and for glory to your people Israel."*

What is fascinating here is how the Spirit of God illumined Simeon to know of and recognize the Messiah and then to proclaim that Christ was the light for revelation, or the illumination, to the Gentiles. Christ's ministry, in a functional sense, can be boiled down to anointed communication; but the Bible does not limit Jesus's communication to mere words. Jesus not only preached a message—he was and is the message. John's Gospel makes this abundantly clear, declaring at the beginning that Jesus is "The true light, which enlightens everyone … coming into the world" (John 1:9). When Jesus preached, the message was really all about him. He himself was the content of all his sermons—he was and is the Savior. He proclaimed himself to be "the light of the world" (8:12), and in so doing, the communicator became the communication of his own sermon.

Illuminated Disciples

Jesus's disciples were also Spirit-illumined communicators. Jesus comforted them by reassuring them that they would not be left without help. He promised that when he left, they would receive the same empowerment to communicate that he had. He said, "But the Helper, the Holy Spirit, whom the Father will send in my name, he will teach you all things and bring to your remembrance all that I have said to you" (John 14:26).

It is significant that the Holy Spirit's operation is connected to truth—here specifically with teaching and remembering truth. It is no accident that the Apostle John referred to the Holy Spirit as "the Spirit of truth" (see, for example, John 15:26; 16:13), confirming the natural link between the Spirit's ministry and revelation. The Spirit is invisible, and he moves where he will (3:8), but this does not mean that the ministry of the Spirit should be understood subjectively as mere feelings or intuition; rather, it is marked by and connected to the Word that he inspired (2 Tim. 3:16). Do not dare to confuse the work of the Spirit with mere human emotions—that is, following emotions as the guide for spiritual life. This is a dangerous trend in the church that takes people off in so many different directions. The Spirit has not left believers to this kind of subjectivity but instead uses the Word of God to provide objective wisdom for all of life's decisions (Josh. 1:8–10; Ps. 119:105; 2 Pet. 1:3).

Illuminated Preachers in the Early Church

This link between the Spirit's ministry and revelation is repeated in the book of Acts in accounts of Spirit-empowered preaching. Time and time again the Spirit of God illumined leaders of the early church to communicate truth and to effect change. Peter's sermon at Pentecost, when he quoted from the Minor Prophet Joel, documented the historic beginning of the New Testament church and showed that what Joel had prophesied was partially being fulfilled. This is what theologians call the "Already/Not Yet" principle. At Pentecost, Peter understood that the Holy Spirit was being poured out in a new and significant way on the early church disciples, and he interpreted what was happening according to Old Testament prophecy:

Acts 2:17–18 *"And in the last days it shall be, God declares,*
that I will pour out my Spirit on all flesh,
and your sons and your daughters shall prophesy,
and your young men shall see visions,
and your old men shall dream dreams;
even on my male servants and female servants in those days
I will pour out my Spirit, and they shall prophesy …"

Peter was given the spiritual discernment to make this connection, and he brought a Spirit-empowered message which in turn brought about massive transformation. Acts 2 recounts this spiritual yield of 3,000 souls who received the Word, were baptized, and were added to the church (v. 41).

Stephen, an early church preacher, was identified as a man "full of grace and power" (Acts 6:8–10). When Stephen went to preach in an eclectic synagogue, the leaders there rose to dispute with him but "they could not withstand the wisdom and the Spirit with which he was speaking" (v. 10). Luke says of Stephen that he was filled with wisdom. It could be said this way: he taught as one filled with the Holy Spirit. He was illumined to speak. The Spirit of God was with Stephen to such an extent that the countenance of this church evangelist shone "like the face of an angel" (v. 15).

Stephen went to preach before Israel's high priest and council, and Acts 7 is the record of his mighty sermon—a sermon he preached with his life on the line. His approach was a simple delivery, and he preached the straight story of redemptive history. He began with the call of Abraham, and from there he unfolded the early biblical record all the way to the coming of Jesus, "the Righteous One" (v. 52). The more he communicated God's character, the more convicted and enraged his hearers became. Ultimately, their rage-filled, hard-hearted response turned this tribunal into a murder scene. Stephen, illumined by the Spirit, responded to their decision to kill him with an incredibly godly focus. Acts records, "But he, full of the Holy Spirit, gazed into heaven and saw the glory of God, and Jesus standing at the right hand of God. And he said, 'Behold, I see the heavens opened, and the Son of Man standing at the right hand of God'" (vv. 55–56).

The Illuminated Preacher

From an account like this, it is clear that the Spirit illumines a man's mind as he is ministering the truth. As we noted earlier, the Apostle Paul was a man who did not trust in his preaching style or methods but rather relied on the simple illumined truth of the Word. The basis of his communication was that he was illumined to believe in truth. Because of this, Paul's preaching method was simple and an example to be followed. Paul summarized this in 2 Corinthians 4:13, where he wrote, "I believed, and so I spoke." Why did Paul preach? The Spirit of God had given him faith, and communication followed. It really is that simple.

The remarkable account in Acts 9 of Paul's conversion illustrates this well. Paul was on his way to Damascus, "breathing threats of murder against the disciples of the Lord" and ready to find all the followers of Jesus to tie them up and haul them back to Jerusalem (vv. 1–2). The Lord intervened: "… suddenly a light from heaven flashed around him" (v. 3). The Lord Jesus knocked Paul to the ground and confronted him, asking, "… why are you persecuting me?" (v. 4). In this account, the light was the presence of the Lord (1 Tim. 6:16), and it was used to blind Paul for three days. Paul's physical blindness was indicative of his spiritual blindness, because at the end of three days, Paul's conversion was evidenced by two things. First, "something like scales fell from his eyes," and second, "he rose and was baptized" (Acts 9:18). Not only could Paul now see physically, but he could also now see spiritually. So, what was Paul's immediate response? He ate some food and "… immediately he proclaimed Jesus in the synagogues, saying, 'He is the Son of God'" (vv. 19–20). He was illumined, and he preached; "I believed, and so I spoke."

What do these passages from Acts 9 have in common? That the preacher is illumined by the truth to speak the truth. His communication is based on illumination. As the passages above reveal, this is the work the Holy Spirit does for the preacher as the preacher interacts with the truth. The one who desires to preach truth must long for the Spirit to illumine his mind. Those who communicate for God must be as passionate as King David was to retain an illumined preaching ministry, literally begging for God's anointing from the Holy Spirit (Ps. 51:11).

Now that we have looked at a few examples of illumined preachers, let's look at a few elements of the illumined preacher's task.

The Preacher's Study

Richard Averbeck, a theological scholar, recognizes how much of biblical teaching today, especially in institutions and seminaries, is dry, perfunctory, and mechanical when the truth does not first inflame the teacher or professor. He believes that biblical scholars and preachers alike need to study, not just to get the biblical message right, but also to be illumined and affected by what is being learned. Averbeck delivers the challenge that "what we need to engage in is the kind of biblical scholarship in which the Bible is not only the subject of investigation, but the investigation itself turns back upon the scholar in a transforming way … [and] this is what illumination is all about" (emphasis added).[25] Averbeck calls scholars to "welcome the Holy Spirit, that

---

[25] Richard E. Averbeck, "God, People, and the Bible: The Relationship between Illumination and Biblical Scholarship," in Daniel B. Wallace and M. James Sawyer, eds., *Who's Afraid of the Holy Spirit? An Investigation into the Ministry of the Spirit of God Today* (Dallas: Biblical Studies Press, 2005), 137.

the Spirit may … do what he intends to do through his word in our study, our lives, and our ministries. This work of the Holy Spirit is sometimes called 'illumination,' the goal of which is to bring the word of God to bear so 'that the eyes of' our 'hearts' may be 'enlightened' (Eph. 1:18; note 'the Spirit of wisdom and revelation' in v. 17 [NIV])."[26]

In other words, the illumined preacher or teacher is called to pass on the very truths about which he was first illumined through personal study. Averbeck speaks insightfully about the fact that "Scholarly study of the Bible can be done either in a way that invites the Holy Spirit to do his transforming work through his word, or in a way that suffocates the work of the Spirit in the scholar's study, and in his or her life and ministry."[27]

Whether they are Old Testament scholars like Averbeck or preachers, those studying the Word of God must study not just to get the biblical message right, but also to be impacted and illumined by what is personally learned. Many preachers think that the Spirit's work of illumination is the rare exception and seem to believe that the Spirit sometimes mystically gives extra insights into the text of Scripture. Not so! The case made by the passages we have examined is that the preacher should expect the ministry of illumination to be a necessary component in his own study and preaching. Again, the "Bible is … the subject of investigation …[which] turns back upon the scholar in a transforming way."[28]

Having this in mind, the Bible student and communicator should maintain that the goal of the study is to have a "transformed life of love from a pure [heart], a good conscience and a sincere faith."[29] He should also approach the study to have an "encounter with God … in submission to the Word."[30] This must culminate with the preacher or teacher "guiding others to read their own Bibles to be affected in the same way the communicator was."[31] The preacher must always have the goal of personal transformation in his mind as he studies the text. When God's Word and his Spirit transform the preacher's heart and actions through study, prayer, and meditation, then and only then can the preacher authentically model the transforming work of illumination to his hearers as the Word is preached. This kind of authenticity does not guarantee that the hearers will be affected, illumined, or transformed (see Chapter 3 on condemnation), but the preacher's conscience can be clear,

---

[26] Ibid., 139.
[27] Ibid.
[28] Ibid., 137.
[29] (1 Tim. 1:5), ibid.
[30] Ibid.
[31] Ibid.

however the Lord chooses to work. Preaching in this way is truly first and foremost a ministry of worship as an offering to God (see Rom. 15:16).

To be an authentic communicator, what is required is diligent study in God's Word and submissiveness to the work of the Spirit in life and ministry. Only then should the preacher expect his preaching to be what John Owen called the "instrumental cause" of conversions and convictions.[32] Preaching is God's biblical method, but to do it right, the preacher must seek authentic illumination.

The Preacher's Message

If we now return to the passage in 2 Corinthians 4 that is central to this discussion of illumination, we see not only how crucial it is for God to first illumine communicators to preach, but also what the Scriptures attest to as the specific method by which the Lord illumines people. What is the actual process whereby God opens blind eyes to see? Paul said in verse 5, "... what we proclaim is not ourselves, but Jesus Christ as Lord, with ourselves as your servants for Jesus' sake."

Paul wanted people to make no mistake about this matter. He wanted his ministry to be viewed in terms of his own self-deprecation. He made it crystal clear that the reason why people believed and saw the glory of Christ was not because Paul promoted himself or his leadership abilities but rather because he promoted the gospel. Paul claims that he did just one thing—he preached "Jesus Christ as Lord." In this way, Paul depicted himself merely as the instrument or tool through which the life-changing message flowed. The change-agent is always the gospel—the message the Apostle Peter called the "imperishable" seed (1 Pet. 1:23).

Paul made this same point in 2 Corinthians 3, saying that the only hope for unbelieving Jews who were "hardened" and unable to make the connection from the old covenant law to Christ was to have their blindness lifted "through Christ" (3:14).

Here is the point: it is only the gospel message, which proclaims that Jesus is Lord, that rips away the veil, allowing a person to "turn to the Lord" (v. 16). Paul knew that there is no human way to change people's hearts—only God's Word can do this work. At the same time, Paul recognized that he was a "jar of clay"—a common household nondescript clay pot that God

---

[32] Owen, *The Holy Spirit*, 137.

designed to contain "treasure" (4:7). Even though Paul, as a clay pot, knew he could never take credit for the heart change that occurred when people came to Christ, he was not passive—he preached (4:5, 13).

Though it is the Word of God that changes people's hearts, the Bible repeatedly asserts that preaching is the dominant functional way by which God communicates truth, enlightening souls trapped in darkness. As we have seen, Paul's testimony attests that as soon as he was illumined, he "immediately … proclaimed Jesus in the synagogues, saying, 'He is the Son of God'" (Acts 9:20).

The Preacher's Vocation

Preaching was Paul's life calling. It was as if this was all he could possibly do. Christ had revealed himself to him, bringing the light of the gospel to his soul, and so Paul gave his entire being to proclaiming this same revelation in order to bring that light to his kinsmen as well as to the Gentiles. Paul spoke of this when he stood before King Agrippa, telling how he had seen "a light from heaven, brighter than the sun" (Acts 26:13). Jesus had revealed himself to Paul, giving Paul his marching orders, saying,

Acts 26:16–18 … *I have appeared to you for this purpose, to appoint you as a servant and witness to the things in which you have seen me and to those in which I will appear to you, delivering you from your people and from the Gentiles—to whom I am sending you to open their eyes, so that they may turn from darkness to light and from the power of Satan to God, that they may receive forgiveness of sins and a place among those who are sanctified by faith in me.*

For Paul, his whole life boiled down to the fact that he was a "witness"; he had seen the resurrected Christ and was appointed to be a spokesman, a communicator of what he had both physically and spiritually seen. Note once again: Paul was called to preach because preaching God's Word opens blind eyes!

Paul continued to describe exactly what his preaching ministry looked like, testifying to King Agrippa, "… O King Agrippa, I was not disobedient to the heavenly vision, but declared first to those in Damascus, then in Jerusalem and throughout all the region of Judea, and also to the Gentiles, that they should repent and turn to God, performing deeds in keeping with their repentance" (vv. 19–20).

Paul used a word here that is synonymous with "preached." He said that he "declared," or "announced," with the purpose of "open[ing] their eyes" and "turn[ing] [his hearers] from darkness to light and from the power of Satan to God" (v. 18). Plain and simple, preaching facilitates illumination.

The Preacher's Preaching

There are two further clear examples of how preaching opened blind eyes. First, there is the example of when Philip preached to the Ethiopian eunuch, who was the high-ranking court official of the queen of the Ethiopians (Acts 8:27). Philip was spiritually led to run up alongside this man's chariot to ask what he was reading. As it turned out, the eunuch was reading about Jesus as the suffering Servant from Isaiah 53. What is interesting is the way Philip asked the question. He said, "Do you understand what you are reading?" (v. 30). Philip was not asking in terms of this man's intellect or comprehension, but in terms of his spiritual apprehension. Throughout Scripture, when a person is said to understand truth, it can most often be equated with spiritual illumination.

This, by the way, is instructive for anyone attempting to evangelize lost people. Evangelism includes asking spiritual questions and listening to the responses. Philip was testing the eunuch to see if the Holy Spirit had illumined him yet. Reading the account, it appears that within that very exchange, the Spirit was indeed opening this man's heart, because he said, "How can I, unless someone guides me?" (v. 31). This showed Philip that the eunuch was open to hear truth, so, as Luke records, "Philip opened his mouth, and beginning with this Scripture, he told him the good news about Jesus" (v. 35). Though this was one-on-one communication, Philip opened his mouth, and the Spirit opened the eunuch's blind eyes.

A second noteworthy example of the communication of truth illumining a person's heart is in Acts 16:13–14. This is the account of how Paul, Silas, and Timothy "… sat down and spoke" to a group of women outside the gate at Philippi. As they did so, one woman named Lydia was converted. Luke recounts that she "heard" the message that was spoken and that "The Lord opened her heart to pay attention to what was said by Paul" (v. 14). On a functional level, Paul spoke the truth, and that was all it took. The Lord took over, opening Lydia's heart "to pay attention to what was said" (v. 14). This is another way of saying she was illumined through preaching to spiritually apprehend the message preached.

The Preacher's Resolve

At this point, we need to remember how important it is to properly understand the nature of the book that preachers are to communicate. Sometimes, when preaching is emphasized, it can be easy to forget that the power of preaching is bound up in the message, not the speech-act. Though it is important to understand the biblical case that the Spirit's involvement is a necessity for the preacher or hearer to be illumined, it is equally crucial to understand the nature of the book the Spirit originally wrote (2 Tim. 3:16; 2 Pet. 1:21). The Bible is a God-inspired book that is meant to communicate. It is not merely what scholars call "locutionary"—that it simply "says something"—but it is "illocutionary,"[33] that is, "it does something."[34] Though the Bible is objective, it is written with the purpose of warning, asserting, and promising.[35] The Bible is also what scholars call "perlocutionary": it is a book addressing real people in real time.[36] It is a book that, by nature, not only informs but also persuades and "invites a response," making it "interlocutionary."[37]

The Bible itself claims to be inspired by the Holy Spirit (2 Tim. 3:16), alive, and powerful (Heb. 4:12). These attributes separate it from every other piece of written material for all time. How freeing it is for the preacher to come to grips with the fact that the Scripture, not the speaker, is the change-agent! The speaker must, of course, do all he can to narrow the distance between the "ancient author" of the text and the "modern reader,"[38] but he must always do this by recognizing that it is the Word that does the work of illumination.

Once again, recognizing the nature of the Scriptures should take pressure off the communicator, because God's Word was written as a book to communicate. The preacher dare not allow himself to cave in to the pressure to overemphasize speaking methodologies from postmodern preachers. Any preaching style or method is, in and of itself, superficial and unable to affect real spiritual change in the hearts of people. The Bible calls for men of God

---

[33] Vanhoozer, *Is There a Meaning in This Text? The Bible, the Reader, and the Morality of Literary Knowledge* (Grand Rapids: Zondervan, 1998), 32–33.

[34] Averbeck, "God, People, and the Bible," 144. Averbeck summarizes Vanhoozer's treatment of speech-act theory as it relates to the ministry of the Holy Spirit and preaching, from Vanhoozer's *Is There a Meaning in This Text?* And "Introduction: Hermeneutics, Text, and Biblical Theology," *in New International Dictionary of Old Testament Theology and Exegesis* (Grand Rapids: Zondervan, 1999).

[35] Vanhoozer, *Is There a Meaning in This Text?*, 410–413.

[36] Ibid.

[37] Ibid.

[38] Averbeck, "God, People, and the Bible," 139–140.

to preach with clarity and simplicity—leaving the Spirit to do his work of opening hearts and allowing people to see the glory of Jesus and his gospel. As Paul told Timothy, "… preach the word" (2 Tim. 4:2). This Word is God's own living and powerful book, inspired and fashioned to communicate.

7

Conversion by Illumination

What are the glorious consequences of faithfully communicating the gospel? Seeing people come to Christ! This is one of the highest joys for any believer, and it is an exciting and unforgettable experience to be used by the Lord as a conduit through whom the Spirit and Word work. Can you remember times when you were used by God to be his mouthpiece to speak words of eternal life to others? It is humbling and inspiring at the same time. It is so easy to fail to make this mission of the gospel a priority, yet giving the gospel—"the ministry of reconciliation" (2 Cor. 5:18)—is one of the primary reasons why Christians are here on earth.

THE ROLE OF GOD'S WORD IN ILLUMINATION

It is clear from 2 Corinthians 4 that it is the Word that ignites illumination in a person's heart, and that believers are often instrumental in this process as they speak the truth. Conversion is the miracle whereby God creates light in a person's soul. Paul testified of his own conversion experience, saying, "For God, who said, 'Let light shine out of darkness,' has shone in our hearts" (v. 6). This describes the Lord's illuminating work in Paul's own heart when he was converted. So, what actually happens when a person is converted—when the lights come on?

Old Testament: New Covenant

There are two important passages in the Old Testament that vividly picture what it looks like when a person is converted. The first passage is the prophet Jeremiah's prophecy of the new covenant, which he describes by saying, "For this is the covenant that I will make with the house of Israel after those days, declares the LORD: I will put my law within them, and I will write it on their hearts. And I will be their God, and they shall be my people" (31:33).

Jeremiah was, at this point in Judah's history, speaking of Israel's and Judah's need for heart transformation. God's nation had failed under the Mosaic covenant, and so God spoke through his prophet to provide the answer to the nation's dilemma, bringing a new covenant of heart change. This was a covenant with Israel and only took effect with the remnant who were granted conversion (Rom. 11:5); however, the new covenant was also applied to the church. Though Jeremiah was not aware of this application of his prophecy, the new covenant is the banner for all conversion that takes place in the New Testament church (2 Cor. 3:6).

Ezekiel is the second prophet who prophesied of this same thing: "And I will give you a new heart, and a new spirit I will put within you. And I will remove the heart of stone from your flesh and give you a heart of flesh. And I will put my Spirit within you, and cause you to walk in my statutes and be careful to obey my rules" (36:26–27). Like Jeremiah, Ezekiel was speaking of spiritual heart transformation for the nation of Israel. His prophecy was pointing to new-covenant heart transformation that is now experienced in the church, whereby "the Spirit gives life" (2 Cor. 3:6).

New Covenant: Same Salvation

In the Gospels, New Testament conversion begins with Jesus. He is repeatedly seen offering the Kingdom, discerning who was truly part of it and who was not. Jesus's disciples were not exempt from being put to this same test. Remember that Jesus questioned the Twelve as to whether they truly knew whom they were following. Jesus asked, "But who do you say that I am?" and Peter, no doubt first to respond, said, "You are the Christ, the Son of the living God" (Matt. 16:15–16). What is interesting is what Jesus discerned from Peter's answer. Jesus said, "Blessed are you, Simon Bar-Jonah! For flesh and blood has not revealed this to you, but my Father who is in heaven" (v. 17). When Jesus declared Peter to be "blessed," he was affirming not only that the Holy Spirit had provided him with the correct answer, but also that Peter had truly been converted. He had a "blessed" spiritual status. Peter was not just another curious follower, still waiting to be convinced that Jesus was the Messiah. His heart had been transformed by illumined revelation.

There were many people following Jesus, watching him preach and perform miracles, whom Jesus discerned were not part of the Kingdom. According to John's Gospel, the Lord was careful not to entrust himself to those who did not truly believe (John 2:24). He knew that genuine conversion was more than an adjustment of a person's will or disposition whereby a person would merely acknowledge Jesus as a powerful speaker or miracle worker. Jesus's ministry always defined conversion as that which comes only by the Spirit of God and which totally transforms a person's heart.

Perhaps the clearest example of this is in John 3, where the Lord met the Pharisee named Nicodemus. Nicodemus set up this meeting with Jesus during the night, perhaps out of fear for his own reputation as a religious leader. He would not want to be seen with Jesus, who was known as a radical. Though Nicodemus affirmed Jesus as a respected rabbi or teacher with a unique connection with God, Jesus discerned that this was a superficial response. Jesus approached him with a test, saying, "Truly, truly, I say to you, unless one is born again he cannot see the kingdom of God" (v. 3). Jesus further clarified this, saying, "That which is born of the flesh is flesh, and that which is born of the Spirit is spirit. Do not marvel that I said to you, 'You must be born again'" (vv. 6–7). By these statements, Jesus showed that being converted by the Spirit of God is as dramatic as being physically born in the first place. He then made it clear that only when a person experiences spiritual conversion does he or she "see the kingdom of God" (v. 3). Jesus was emphatic with Nicodemus about the Spirit's essential role in conversion.

Again, in John 6, knowing that the crowds were seeking his miracles more than they were seeking him, Jesus said, "It is the Spirit who gives life; the flesh is no help at all. The words that I have spoken to you are spirit and life" (v. 63). Jesus was clear that no amount of human effort will give anybody spiritual life since "the flesh is no help at all." However, when the Holy Spirit opens a person's heart, the words of Jesus become "spirit and life." It is the Spirit of God energizing the Word that converts those who are blind, causing them to see.

ILLUMINED BY THE WORD

The radical conversion of the Apostle Paul is a striking example of spiritual conversion. He was a man transformed by the power of the Holy Spirit and by the revelation of Jesus. Prior to conversion, Paul was known for being "a persecutor of the church" (Phil. 3:6) and "a blasphemer, persecutor, and insolent opponent" (1 Tim. 1:13). To top it all off, he called himself "the foremost" of sinners (v. 15). His conversion was unique and obviously different in at least two ways from the conversion a person experiences today:

his conversion included the calling to be an apostle, and this required him to be an eyewitness of the resurrected Christ (Acts 26:16; 1 Cor. 9:1). Even so, there is overlap with what all believers experience, specifically regarding illumination. All who are saved are illumined. Note again Paul's testimony in Acts 9, but this time in terms of his conversion. Luke wrote,

Acts 9:3–5 *Now as he went on his way, he approached Damascus, and suddenly a light from heaven shone around him. And falling to the ground, he heard a voice saying to him, "Saul, Saul, why are you persecuting me?" And he said, "Who are you, Lord?" And he said, "I am Jesus, whom you are persecuting.*

There is some debate as to whether Paul's conversion took place when the Lord confronted him in verses 3–5 or later when Ananias met him in Damascus. The strongest evidence that Paul's conversion happened on the road to Damascus is that there the Lord commissioned him to be an apostle to the Gentiles. Paul's testimony confirms this. Paul quoted Jesus as having said,

Acts 26:16–18 ... *I have appeared to you for this purpose, to appoint you as a servant and witness to the things in which you have seen me and to those in which I will appear to you, delivering you from your people and from the Gentiles—to whom I am sending you to open their eyes, so that they may turn from darkness to light and from the power of Satan to God, that they may receive forgiveness of sins and a place among those who are sanctified by faith in me.*

The scriptural support for the position that Paul's conversion occurred later is found in the context of Acts 9, when he met with Ananias. It is recorded that "something like scales fell from his eyes" (v. 18), which could symbolize either the illuminating work of the Spirit that had already taken place on the road to Damascus or the work that was taking place at that moment with Ananias in Damascus.

THE ROLE OF THE SPIRIT IN ILLUMINATION

From Acts 9, we can identify three features that Paul's conversion has in common with the conversions of all believers everywhere.

Transformed by the Word

First, spiritual conversion involves dramatic transformation. This is impossible to miss from the account of Paul's conversion. Of course, knowing Paul's pre-conversion state highlights this, and in some ways causes his conversion to stand out as a more remarkable example than most. Remember who Paul was? Paul was transformed from chief persecutor of Christians to chief apostle. He stood out among the Pharisees for the fervor with which he captured and sanctioned death sentences for all those "belonging to the Way" (Acts 9:2).

Paul, himself later persecuted for his faith, testified of his own participation in the martyrdom of the evangelist Stephen. He was not merely present when Stephen's blood was shed, but was functioning as supervisor, "… standing by and approving and watching over the garments of those who killed him" (Acts 22:20). The Jerusalem church knew his reputation well, having heard so much about this zealous young Pharisee. They knew so much about him that they did not immediately trust him. When Paul turned up to "join the disciples … they were all afraid of him, for they did not believe that he was a disciple" (9:26).

As extraordinary of a conversion as this was, the Bible teaches that all true conversions, from a spiritual standpoint, are extraordinary. Even though from a human (and therefore surface) perspective Paul's testimony and conversion experience appear more dramatic than those of the average believer, all conversions are acts of God. In all conversions, people are "… delivered … from the domain of darkness and transferred … to the kingdom of his beloved Son" (Col. 1:13).

No matter how it looks from the human vantage point, each conversion is amazing. Paul is emphatic in Romans 1:16 that the "gospel" is the "power of God for salvation to everyone who believes." All newly converted people have had "the righteousness of God … revealed" to them by faith (v. 17), which again comes back to the work of the Holy Spirit, who opens blind eyes to grasp the truth and glory of the gospel.

Hearing the Word

A second commonality between Paul's conversion and all conversions is the revelation of truth by the Holy Spirit. Note how Paul testified of this when he wrote to the churches of Galatia: "For I would have you know, brothers, that the gospel that was preached by me is not man's gospel. For I did not receive it from any man, nor was I taught it, but I received it through a revelation of Jesus Christ" (1:11–12). Paul placed his preaching ministry in the background to emphasize that the power to transform souls came solely from the gospel message itself. What he preached was "not man's gospel"— not something contrived by a mere man—but instead "received … through a revelation of Jesus Christ." Paul received direct revelation from Christ, but all believers are illumined by the Holy Spirit as to the truth of Jesus Christ; all have Jesus revealed to them.

Receiving the Word

A third commonality of all conversions is this: when Paul spoke of receiving revelation, he was not referring to seeing Christ with his eyes (even though he did in fact see him) but to hearing him with his ears. Remember from Acts 9:3–5 that Paul was blinded by the glorious flash of light around him and that "… falling to the ground he heard a voice" which said, "I am Jesus." Paul's conversion came from hearing the truth of the gospel. He said the same thing to the Romans when he wrote to them that people see spiritually by hearing the truth: "… faith comes from hearing, and hearing through the word of Christ" (10:17). When a person's eyes are opened to embrace Jesus, he or she does not need one shred of extra-biblical or historical evidence to seal the deal. There is no need for evidential apologetics. Whether or not the new believer understands it at that point in time, the gospel is what has saved him or her, not a personal cerebral convincing of the truth. The gospel is always what reveals Jesus. John Piper said it this way:

> Jesus, as he is revealed in the Bible, has a glory—an excellence, a spiritual beauty—that can be seen as self-evidently true. It is like seeing the sun and knowing that it is light and not dark, or like tasting honey and knowing that it is sweet and not sour … How can they know him and be sure of him? What they "see" is the verbal portrayal of Jesus in the Gospel, that is, in the apostolic preaching of Christ.[39]

You Can't Believe What You Haven't Heard

Conversion comes through hearing words of truth, hearing this "verbal portrayal of Jesus." Whether a person reads the Word and hears it in his or her mind, or actually hears words spoken aloud to his or her physical ears, this is the way it happens for anybody who has ever been converted.[40]

Back in 2 Corinthians 4, conversion is described as an act of the Creator. Simply put, God creates light in people's hearts. Remember that Paul drew a direct parallel between God as the creator of physical light—"For God, who said, 'Let light shine out of darkness'"—and God as the creator of spiritual light—"has shone in our hearts to give the light of the knowledge of the glory of God in the face of Jesus Christ" (v. 6). This is the picture of what happens

---

[39] John Piper, *Seeing and Savoring Jesus Christ* (Wheaton, IL: Crossway, 2004), 119–20.
[40] Ibid., 120.

in the heart when someone is converted. A person held captive in spiritual darkness by sin and Satan is suddenly enlightened to see God's glory "in the face of Jesus."

This is a work in which God "awakens [people], as from the dead, to see and taste the divine reality of God in Scripture, which authenticates it as God's own word."[41] Conversion is "the immediate, unassailable, life-giving revelation to the mind of the majesty of God manifest in the Scriptures themselves."[42] Under this banner, "Illumination … in principle [is] that gift granted to the child of God, from the very moment of his new birth, which permits him to see the kingdom of God (John 3:3) … [and which is] normally permanent and increasing."[43] Jonathan Edwards summarized a believer's new perspective thus: "Things that appertain to the way of salvation by Christ are opened to him in a new manner, and he now understands those divine and spiritual doctrines which once were foolishness to him."[44] The Word of God makes it unmistakably clear that a person's conversion is entirely the work of God. Piper put it this way:

… God witnesses to us of his reality and the reality of his Son and his Word by giving us life from the dead so that we come alive to his majesty and see him for who he is in his Word. In that instant we do not reason from premises to conclusions, we see that we are awake, and there is not even a prior human judgment about it to lean on. When Lazarus wakened in the tomb by the call or the "witness" of Christ, he knew without reasoning that he was alive and that this call wakened him [emphasis added].[45]

The Spirit-Empowered Preacher

What impact does understanding the doctrine of illumination in conversion have upon the preacher? The power of conversion is the power of the Holy Spirit bringing light to a blind soul through the Word of God. The power of conversion is the Holy Spirit raising a soul from spiritual death (Eph. 2:5), bringing someone to life spiritually. God invades a soul enthralled

---

[41] John Piper, "The Divine Majesty of the Word: John Calvin, The Man and His Preaching," Bethlehem Conference for Pastors, February 4, 1997, https://www.desiringgod.org/messages/the-divine-majesty-of-the-word.
[42] Ibid.
[43] René Pache, Helen I. Needham, tr., *The Inspiration and Authority of Scripture* (Salem, WI: Sheffield Publishing, 1969; 1992), 199.
[44] Edwards, *The Religious Affections*, 193.
[45] Piper, *The Divine Majesty of the Word*.

by sin and darkness and sets it free, bringing the light of faith (Rom. 1:17). It is wholly of God, wholly by the Spirit's ministry of illumination.

Just as the Word of God faithfully preached brings condemnation to some, so it brings life to others. The Spirit works in concert with the Word and brings illumination to some so that they are able to hear, with spiritual ears opened, and understand, with hearts enlightened by faith.

Preach the Word, knowing that the Spirit will work. Preach the Word—God will harden some hearts and illumine others. Preach the Word and know, as did the faithful preachers throughout the Bible, that the Lord will give life, will open hearts, and will transfer people from the kingdom of darkness to the "kingdom of his beloved Son" (Col. 1:13).

8

Convictions through Illumination

In 1 Corinthians 2:14, Paul wrote, "The natural person does not accept the things of the Spirit of God, for they are folly to him, and he is not able to understand them because they are spiritually discerned." There is some debate as to what Paul meant when he said that "the things of the Spirit" are "folly" or "foolishness." Some believe he was saying that unbelievers, since they do not have the Holy Spirit, have no capacity to cognitively understand the fundamental meaning of Scripture. The Bible is therefore "folly" because it doesn't make sense to unspiritual people. Others state that what Paul meant was that unbelievers, devoid of the Holy Spirit, are unable to gain spiritual convictions about the truthfulness, authority, and significance of Scripture, and see biblical truth as "folly."[46]

CONVICTED BY THE SPIRIT

Martin Luther supported the second perspective. He believed that there is what he called an "outer and an inner clarity of Scripture."[47] The outer, or external, clarity means that "by the usual laws or rules of language a Christian could understand the Scripture as a written document."[48] However, "Due to man's sinfulness he needs an inward assist so that he might grasp the spiritual Word of God as the Word of God. The Word of God is a spiritual entity and can only be understood in faith with the help of the Holy Spirit."[49] This is what he called the "inner clarity of Scripture," and for Luther, the Holy Spirit

---

[46] Heisler, *Spirit-Led Preaching*, 46.
[47] Bernard L. Ramm, *Rapping about the Spirit* (Waco, TX: Word, 1974), 84.
[48] Ibid.
[49] Ibid.

in this role "was the Hermes from heaven."[50] Christians need a lamp for their convictions.

Imprinted Convictions

John Calvin called this phenomenon of illumination "imprinting." In the answer to question 302 of his Geneva Catechism, he said that this spiritual work happens when we receive the text of Scripture "… with the full consent of our conscience, as truth comes down from heaven, submitting ourselves to it in right obedience, loving it with true affection by having it imprinted in our hearts, [so that] we may follow it entirely and conform ourselves to it" (emphasis added).[51] This is where the Word obtains "… acceptance in men's hearts, before it is sealed by the inward testimony of the Spirit."[52] In this way a believer affirms the Word "… with utter certainty (just as if we were gazing upon the majesty of God himself) that it [the Word] has flowed to us from the very mouth of God by the ministry of men."[53]

Transforming Convictions

The work of the Spirit Calvin describes as "imprinting" is sometimes referred to by scholars as "impressing." Note how the modern scholar Kevin Vanhoozer used this terminology:

> The Spirit illumines the letter by impressing its illocutionary force on the reader. Thanks to the illumination of the Spirit, we see and hear speech acts for what they are—warnings, promises, commands, assertions—together with their implicit claim in our minds and hearts. In so doing, the Spirit does not alter but ministers the meaning: "The spiritual sense is the literal sense correctly understood." The distinction between "letter" and "spirit" is precisely that between reading words and grasping what one reads. Likewise, the difference between a "natural" and an "illuminated" understanding is that

---

[50] Ibid.

[51] John Calvin, "Geneva Catechism," in Thomas F. Torrance, ed. and tr., *The School of Faith: The Catechisms of the Reformed Church* (Eugene, OR: Wipf and Stock, 1959), 52–53.

[52] John Calvin, Ford Lewis Battles tr., *Calvin: Institutes of the Christian Religion*, vols. XX and XXI of John Baillie, John T. McNeill, and Henry P. Van Dusen, eds., The Library of Christian Classics (Louisville, KY: Westminster John Knox Press, 1960), 79.

[53] Ibid., 80.

between holding an opinion and having a deep sense of its profundity."[54]

Likewise, note Greg Heisler's definition: "Illumination is the process whereby the Holy Spirit so impresses, convinces, and convicts the believer as to the truthfulness and significance of the author's intended meaning in the text that a change in action, attitude, or belief occurs, resulting in a more transformed, Spirit-filled life."[55]

Illumined Convictions

How does the Bible depict the gaining of spiritual convictions? First comes conversion, in which a person is initially illumined by the Spirit and revelation. At justification, having been illumined, such a person has gained a crucial part of progressive sanctification: spiritual convictions.

This is bound up in a simple phrase found back in 2 Corinthians 4. There, Paul described a person's initial illumination, saying that light "... has shone in our hearts to give the light of the knowledge of the glory of God in the face of Jesus Christ" (v. 6). When a person is converted or initially illumined, he or she gains what Paul simply called "knowledge." It is clear that, by using this term, he was not talking about academic data. Charles Hodge wrote of this knowledge:

> The other truth here taught is, that this knowledge of God in Christ is not a mere matter of intellectual apprehension, which one man may communicate to another. It is a spiritual discernment, to be derived only from the Spirit of God. God must shine into our hearts to give us this knowledge. Matt. 16:17; Gal. 1:16; 1 Cor. 2:10, 14. As the glory of God is spiritual, it must be spiritually discerned. It is therefore easy to see why the Scriptures make true religion to consist in the knowledge of Christ, and why they make the denial of Christ, or want of faith in him as God manifest in the flesh, a soul-destroying sin.[56]

The context of 2 Corinthians 4 speaks of "knowledge" as Spirit-wrought convictions regarding spiritual truth. The Spirit makes the impression on the

---

[54] Kevin J. Vanhoozer, *Is There a Meaning in This Text?*, 413.
[55] Heisler, *Spirit-Led Preaching*, 43. Heisler's definition is based upon the work of Robert H. Stein in his book *Playing by the Rules: A Basic Guide to Interpreting the Bible* (Grand Rapids: Baker, 1994).
[56] Charles Hodge, *Commentary on the Second Epistle to the Corinthians* (Grand Rapids: Eerdmans, 1864; n.d.), 91.

heart that biblical truth is true. Convincing someone of the absolute certainty of spiritual truth is a work only God can achieve. Paul's Spirit-illumined convictions shaped his entire life—everything he did, spoke, and sacrificed came back to this. He was willing to stake his whole life on what he believed.

Nowhere is this more clearly seen than in what Paul wrote immediately after 2 Corinthians 4:1–6:

2 Cor. 4:8–14 *We are afflicted in every way, but not crushed; perplexed, but not driven to despair; persecuted, but not forsaken; struck down, but not destroyed; always carrying in the body the death of Jesus, so that the life of Jesus may also be manifested in our bodies. For we who live are always being given over to death for Jesus' sake, so that the life of Jesus also may be manifested in our mortal flesh. So death is at work in us, but life in you. Since we have the same spirit of faith according to what has been written, "I believed, and so I spoke," we also believe, and so we also speak, knowing that he who raised the Lord Jesus will raise us also with Jesus and bring us with you into his presence.*

For Paul, it was simple. Because he had been illumined to see Jesus, he was willing to face horrible persecution and suffering, living as he did under the equivalent of a death sentence. He lived his life as a walking target for Christ-hating persecutors. This text says that he was comforted, knowing that God was using his sacrifice to bring spiritual life to others (v. 12). He lived his life absolutely convinced of this.

In summarizing the power of these spiritual convictions which he possessed, he took a quote from the psalmist to characterize his entire preaching ministry. Paul said, "Since we have the same spirit of faith according to what has been written, 'I believed, and so I spoke,' we also believe, and so we also speak" (v. 13, quoting Ps. 116:10). Paul was simply saying that he lived just like the prophets of old—men who believed truth in a way that drove them to preach no matter the consequences (see Heb. 11:32–38). In other words, the reality of Paul's Spirit-illumined convictions meant he could not contain himself. He was driven to proclaim what he believed—his convictions—to anyone who would listen.

The Source of Convictions

Verse 14 tells us exactly what convictions he was referring to, again with the word "knowing" (compare "knowledge" in 2 Cor. 4:6). His conviction was the gospel: "knowing that he who raised the Lord Jesus will raise us also with Jesus and bring us with you into his presence." What made Paul a zealous radical preacher—a madman by the world's standards? He suffered and preached because he was certain that, just as God raised Jesus from the dead, he too would be raised from death with Jesus to be in the Father's presence. This truth, this treasure, was worth giving his life for. Only when a person is illumined and filled with conviction will he then or she follow Jesus in the way in which Jesus calls people to follow him (Matt. 16:24).

Paul knew that he was nothing special. He did not have some extra measure of illumined convictions. This is why he said, "we also believe, and so we also speak" (2 Cor. 4:13) and included all believers, knowing they possessed the same convictions. He gave the same kind of affirmation when he said that he knew the Thessalonians were "chosen" by God because of the way they received the gospel "not only in word, but also in power and in the Holy Spirit and with full conviction" (1 Thess. 1:4–5). In his second letter to the Thessalonians, Paul again gave thanks "because God chose" them "to be saved," and here he moved beyond their salvation experience to their sanctification, saying it was "... by the Spirit and belief in the truth" (2 Thess. 2:13). These statements tell how the members of this church were certain, and growing in the certainty, of their beliefs.

Spirit-illumined convictions are always the mark of genuine salvation. Paul's prayer to Timothy was that he would gently correct opponents of the gospel so that "God may perhaps grant them repentance leading to a knowledge of the truth" (2 Tim. 2:25). When a person repents or turns from sin (see 1 Thess. 1:9), he or she gains and begins to grow in Spirit-illumined convictions, or, as Paul said, in "a knowledge of the truth." Paul launched the epistle of Titus by characterizing his entire apostolic ministry as being "for the sake of the faith of God's elect and their knowledge of the truth, which accords with godliness" (Titus 1:1). As with the 2 Timothy passage, the phrase "knowledge of the truth" represents convictions, but here, believers gain them at salvation for the purpose of their sanctification or "godliness" (v. 1), as was the case with the Thessalonians. So, whether a person is a brand-new believer repenting of sin for the first time, or a decades-old believer still growing in godliness, each possesses spiritually illumined convictions called the "knowledge of the truth."

Illumined convictions found in a believer's salvation and sanctification are indicative of spiritual appetite. When the psalmist cried out, "Oh, taste and see that the LORD is good!" (34:8), this was what he was talking about. In this context, "taste" pictures a person whose soul is filled by the Lord's goodness. Another way to say this is that a person knows—is convinced—that God is good, and he or she is affected or moved by it. The Apostle Peter encouraged this kind of spiritual hunger, saying believers should be like "new-born infants" who "long for the pure spiritual milk" in order to grow spiritually (1 Pet. 2:2). Peter described what should be the norm for someone who has "tasted that the Lord is good" (v. 3) at conversion. It is only natural that, once a person knows that something tastes good, he or she will want more of it. This is how appetite works. A spiritual appetite of this nature is the reason why men of God have, just like the psalmist, begged God, saying, "Open my eyes, that I may behold wondrous things out of your law" (119:18). Those with this kind of hunger long for "unveiled discernment, 20/20 spiritual perception" when they read the truth.[57] Their illumined convictions drive them back for more.

Time Tested Convictions

Some might assume that, since the New Testament says much more about the Holy Spirit than the Old Testament, illumination is primarily a New Testament doctrine. It is easy to forget that Old Testament saints were also illumined by the Spirit of God and had the same kind of spiritual appetites as their New Testament counterparts. The Spirit's involvement in illumining saints may not be as clear in the Old Testament as it is in the New, but from what is known in the New Testament, it is not difficult to infer what was happening for Old Testament believers.

As a first example, let's look in the book of Job, the oldest book of the Bible, to catch a small glimpse of illumination. At the end of the book, the LORD confronts Job after he has gone through the unbelievable trial of having all his children struck dead and all his wealth stripped away almost instantaneously. Job was struggling to persevere in faith. One of the ways the Lord exhorted him was by reminding him of who had opened his mind to truth in the first place. The LORD asked him this question: "Who has put wisdom in the inward parts or given understanding to the mind?" (38:36).

Though this example only gives a glimpse at Old Testament illumination, the book of Psalms is much more explicit on the subject. The psalmist says many times that God has opened his mind to grasp spiritual truths. In Psalm 19, the psalmist extolled the Word of God, saying:

Ps. 19:7–8 *The law of the LORD is perfect,*
reviving the soul;
the testimony of the LORD is sure,
making wise the simple;
the precepts of the LORD are right,

---

[57] George J. Zemek, *The Word of God in the Child of God: Exegetical, Theological, and Homiletical Reflections from the 119th Psalm* (Mango, FL: n.p.; n.d.), 103.

rejoicing the heart;
the commandment of the LORD is pure,
  enlightening the eyes.

Here, he declared the convictions that he had regarding the Word of God. He was emphatic that the Word is "perfect," or sound and without error, and that that was what resuscitated his soul. He also spoke of its impeccable testimony and its ability to provide wisdom for the simplest believer. He asserted that the Word is truthful and joy-creating, clean and uncontaminated, and, finally, that it illumines the eyes.

What causes a person to see the Bible in this way? This Old Testament saint did not gain these convictions by scientific, historical, linguistic, or any other academic or interpretive means. This man's eyes were enlightened by the truth itself, by seeing what is so wonderful about this truth. Psalm 119 repeats this same dynamic over and over, saying that the Bible illumines believers to hunger for and love it. These are just a few of the highlights:

- "Make me understand the way of your precepts, and I will meditate on your wondrous works" (v. 27).

- "Your hands have made and fashioned me; give me understanding that I may learn your commandments" (v. 73).

- "Oh how I love your law! It is my meditation all the day. Your commandment makes me wiser than my enemies, for it is ever with me. I have more understanding than all my teachers, for your testimonies are my meditation. I understand more than the aged, for I keep your precepts" (vv. 97–100).

- "How sweet are your words to my taste, sweeter than honey to my mouth! Through your precepts I get understanding; therefore I hate every false way. Your word is a lamp to my feet and a light to my path" (vv. 103–105).

- "The unfolding of your words gives light; it imparts understanding to the simple" (v. 130).

- "Your testimonies are righteous forever; give me understanding that I may live" (v. 144).

- "The sum of your word is truth, and every one of your righteous rules endures forever" (v. 160).

- "Let my cry come before you, O LORD; give me understanding according to your word!" (v. 169).

Much like the psalmist, the prophet Jeremiah had the Word of God revealed to him. These revelations in turn became his convictions. This is pictured by his expression of his appetite, his spiritual hunger for the Word of God, when he said, "Your words were found, and I ate them, and your words became to me a joy and the delight of my heart ..." (15:16).

Correcting Your Convictions by God's Word

There is a very clear example in the Gospel of Luke of two late-coming disciples of Christ who were suddenly illumined with convictions. This is the account in Luke 24:13–35 of how Jesus, having just been raised from the dead, met two men on the road to Emmaus. These two were extremely discouraged because, in their minds, their hopes for redemption had been dashed. They believed that their would-be Messiah, Jesus, had failed. The coup that they had hoped would overthrow Rome's rule over their nation was not going to happen. Jesus had been killed (vv. 19–21).

As he often did, Jesus took a very direct approach with these two, calling them "foolish ones ... [who were] slow of heart to believe all that the prophets have spoken!" (v. 25). It is amazing to see the way Jesus moved from his rebuke to his revelation. He did not leave these two lost in confusion, but went on to explain himself from the Scriptures: "'Was it not necessary that the Christ should suffer these things and enter into his glory?' And beginning with Moses and all the Prophets, he interpreted to them in all the Scriptures the things concerning himself" (vv. 26–27). Christ Jesus did not appeal to his own authority to reveal himself; he appealed to the written Word of God. Since he was standing right in front of them, it would have been so easy for him just to say, "Don't you get it? I'm the one who rose from the dead! I'm Jesus the Messiah!" Instead, however, "he interpreted ... the Scriptures ... concerning himself" (v. 27). Here, the Son of God was seen expositing the Old Testament Scriptures that pointed to his own coming, with the purpose of revealing himself.

By appealing to the Old Testament text, at least the Pentateuch and Prophets, Jesus showed by example what illumines a heart. This is such a grand testimony to the power of the Word of God! As the story goes, the more these disciples heard Jesus's expository teaching, the more they wanted to hear. When Jesus looked as if he might leave, they begged him to stay into the evening. After teaching them for some time, just as they began to eat supper, something amazing happened: these disciples had their "eyes … opened, and they recognized [Jesus]" (v. 31). At this point, Jesus vanished, but these men recognized where the illumination came from—the Scriptures. This is clear from their response: "Did not our hearts burn within us while he talked to us on the road, while he opened to us the Scriptures?" (v. 32). Their hearts burned within them, their affections resonated deeply with what Jesus was explaining, "while he opened to [them] the Scriptures." This is a picture of the Spirit of God making his deep mark on the human heart through the agency of the Word of God as it is explained. Jonathan Edwards, commenting on this narrative, said, "When Christ makes the Scripture a means of the heart's burning with gracious affection, it is by opening the Scriptures to their understanding."[58]

Another example is when Jesus appeared to his eleven apostles and disciples in Jerusalem. It seems reasonable to expect that he would have received a better reception from this group. Unlike the two Jesus met on the road to Emmaus, these were his intimate friends and companions. If anyone could be expected to recognize Jesus and understand what was happening, surely it would be them! Instead, when Jesus appeared to them, rather than them immediately embracing him as the risen Son of God, they were "startled," "frightened," "troubled," had "doubts arise in [their] hearts," and "still disbelieved" (Luke 24:37–41). It was not until they were illumined that they were sure who he was. Luke records that Jesus "… said to them, 'These are my words that I spoke to you while I was still with you, that everything written about me in the Law of Moses and the Prophets and the Psalms must be fulfilled.' Then he opened their minds to understand the Scriptures" (vv. 44–45). Once again, Jesus used Scripture as the means of opening their minds. Just as before, he appealed to the Old Testament to show that the plan had all along been for the Christ to go to the cross and rise from the dead on the third day (vv. 44–47). Once illumined, his disciples were now certain of this.

CONVICTING LETTERS

The Spirit's role of illumining believers to have convictions is also a significant theme throughout the epistles. In Romans 8, Paul put the topic of spiritual illumination in the context of mortifying sin. Look at Romans 8:13–16:

---

[58] Edwards, *The Religious Affections*, 194.

Rom. 8:13–16 *For if you live according to the flesh you will die, but if by the Spirit you put to death the deeds of the body, you will live. For all who are led by the Spirit of God are sons of God. For you did not receive the spirit of slavery to fall back into fear, but you have received the Spirit of adoption as sons, by whom we cry, "Abba! Father!" The Spirit himself bears witness with our spirit that we are children of God ...*

Notice how Paul described illumination. He saw it as taking place when a believer's spirit, or inner man, resonates with the Holy Spirit—when the believer has assurance of his or her salvation, the spiritual conviction that he or she is a child of God. The wonderful point of this text is this: since Christians are illumined, they are given assurance to obey the Lord, not out of fear, as if they are slaves under an evil master, but instead as adopted children responding to a loving father. Paul says that it is conviction emblazoned upon the heart that motivates believers to kill sin in their lives (v. 13)!

It is so much easier to walk in sanctification, obeying the Lord, when we are certain of our status as children of God. Christians who do not have this conviction can easily fall into the trap of being moralistic, attempting to be holy by hard work alone. Under the weight of moralism, the Christian experience becomes drudgery. Paul knew this, which is why he appealed to our adopted status to combat the nasty sin of legalism (cf. Gal. 4:6).

Christ-Minded Convictions

It is worthwhile to focus now on one key phrase in 1 Corinthians 2:16: Paul affirms that believers have "the mind of Christ" (v. 16). For Paul, being illumined is tantamount to having "the mind of Christ." When Paul says this, he is not espousing some form of mysticism, some kind of ethereal mindset that transcends normal thinking.

As demonstrated so far, illumination is always connected to truth and its certainty. In the context of 1 Corinthians 2:12–13, Paul is arguing that there is a contrast between people who think like the world and people who think spiritually. Believers "have received not the spirit of the world, but the Spirit who is from God, that we might understand the things freely given us by God" (v. 12). And what is it that the Spirit helps us to understand? What are "the things freely given us by God?"

In verse 13, Paul says that this is the truth which came through the apostles as "words ... taught by the Spirit." This is the inspired Word of God that is imprinted by the Spirit on the soul of the believer. This is what Paul means by believers having the "mind of Christ." Believers with illumined convictions have spiritual discernment; even though those not illumined might, on a surface level, affirm the Bible, according to Paul, they will, deep down, view it as "folly" with no veracity (v. 14).

Perhaps one of the clearest passages on this aspect of illumination providing spiritual convictions is Ephesians 1:17–18. A study of Ephesians shows that one of Paul's chief motives for writing this letter was so that this church could spiritually recognize, see, and comprehend salvation in terms of its present and future implications. A quick perusal of the letter reveals that Paul did not write it in order to right wrongs that were going on at the church in Ephesus. This epistle is not a polemical treatise but is heavenly-minded and was written to encourage the church to grasp the spiritual riches it had received from God.

In this passage, Paul stated this banner motivation for everything else he wrote in his epistle: "… that the God of our Lord Jesus Christ, the Father of glory, may give you a spirit of wisdom and of revelation in the knowledge of him, having the eyes of your hearts enlightened, that you may know what is the hope to which he has called you, what are the riches of his glorious inheritance in the saints …" Having heard of this church's faith in Jesus and their love for fellow Christians, his affection exploded into his prayer for them (vv. 15–16).

This prayer shows a great deal of his heart, because he prayed this cease-lessly (v. 16). His prayer was really quite simple. He wanted God to illumine their minds to spiritual realities. He was praying this on the basis of their hearts having already been enlightened (v. 18). Incidentally, in this context, the word "enlightened" would be interchangeable with the term "illumi-nated" (this is the case in Heb. 10:32 in the New King James Version—the same Greek term is there translated "illuminated").

Illuminated Wisdom

Paul was desperate for this church to have illumined convictions over spiritual truths. He demonstrated this by using two key phrases: "a spirit of wisdom," and "revelation in the knowledge of him" (v. 17). To be clear about what Paul was praying for in these phrases, note that these categories are not just temporal gifts that were only for certain believers in the early church.

First Corinthians 12:7 says, "To each is given the manifestation of the Spirit for the common good," but then verse 8 says, "For to one is given through the Spirit … wisdom, and to another … knowledge." In verse 7, everyone receives a gift, but in verse 8 there are particular gifts of wisdom and knowledge that not everyone receives. These are for particular believers.

What Paul was praying for in Ephesians 1:17, therefore, was that the whole church would receive this blessing of the spirit of wisdom and the knowledge of God—that all believers, with no exceptions, would have this blessing.

Note also that though the "spirit of wisdom" and "revelation" should be taken as categorically separate, they still go hand in hand. They could be viewed as interlocking rings, something like the Olympic rings. Paul wanted the church he loved to possess spiritual "wisdom," which is synonymous with spiritual discernment. It is simply being able to grasp, to comprehend, spiritual realities. He also wanted them to have "revelation," by which he referred to spiritual realities that would not be revealed to a non-spiritually minded person.

This word "revelation" implies that a truth or spiritual reality must be unveiled or revealed by the Spirit of God. It is also important to understand that "spirit" here is not referring to the Holy Spirit, but instead to the human spirit or the inner man. In other words, God provides "wisdom and … revelation" in the believer's inner man or mind.

The immediate context of Ephesians 1 shows that the foundation for Paul's prayer was that the people in this church had been regenerated. In effect, this means that spiritual convictions are like building blocks, built upon the Spirit's initial transforming work that takes place when he saves a person. In his New Testament commentary on Ephesians, John Calvin explained what Paul was saying here. From a grammatical perspective, Calvin understood Paul to be speaking of "a spirit of wisdom and of revelation" by use of metonymy, which restates a concept similarly but not exactly.[59] In this context, Paul used it by first stating that these believers "… were sealed with the promised Holy Spirit" (v. 13), which is the cause; he then followed this with the effect: the believers would gain "a spirit of wisdom and of revelation" (v. 17).

This is also apparent in Paul's phrase "having the eyes of your hearts enlightened" (v. 18). Instead of this being part of his prayer request for illumination, Paul was affirming what they already had: a spiritual foundation (see v. 13). The phrase "eyes of your hearts" refers to the mind or inner man. This is a person's seat of affections and thinking, and in this context, Paul was writing about that which the Lord spiritually transforms when a person

---

[59] John Calvin, T. H. L. Parker, tr., *The Epistles of Paul the Apostle to the Galatians, Ephesians, Philippians and Colossians*, vol. ii of David W. Torrance and Thomas F. Torrance, eds., Calvin's New Testament Commentaries (Grand Rapids: Eerdmans, 1965), 134.

first believes. This word "enlightened," a perfect passive participle, also tells us that this is God turning the lights on, which occurs at salvation.

This is the cause or foundation for more illumination. New Testament scholar Homer A. Kent commented in a similar way about this text, saying, "To have such awareness, it was absolutely imperative that … [the Ephesians] be spiritually enlightened in their hearts.… This had occurred at regeneration … 'having been enlightened' [which] denotes the present condition resulting from a past act."[60]

In this case, therefore, perhaps a better translation of verses 17–18 would be along the lines of "since the eyes of your hearts have been enlightened … I want you to have spiritual wisdom and revelation." This is what made Paul's request legitimate. He was affirming their capacity to perceive spiritual realities just as a person perceives normal physical life through the five physical senses (see Titus 3:4–6).

As previously noted, Paul mentioned this same reality in 1 Corinthians 2 when he compared the "natural" person with the "spiritual" person (vv. 14–15). The spiritual person, someone already regenerate, has built-in discernment to grasp spiritual realities. It is only this person who can grasp "spiritual truths" (v. 13).

Whose Convictions?

What are the spiritual truths that become convictions? Remember that being given a "spirit of wisdom and of revelation" isn't a mystical effect but is grounded in objective truth—"in the knowledge of him" (Eph. 1:17). These spiritual truths are simply knowledge sourced in God himself. It is knowledge that is unique to the sphere of God. When Paul used the word "knowledge," he was speaking of spiritual convictions rather than of academic or cerebral knowledge. It is knowing about what God knows about, or as Paul said elsewhere, it is having "the mind of Christ" (1 Cor. 2:16).

In general, this is simply reading Scripture with an illumined mind. What is refreshing about this is that Paul's prayer was not solely for those with superior thinking abilities, or solely for those in spiritual leadership; all believers have access to illumination. Charles Hodge, commenting on this "knowledge," said, "It is something which all believers need, and for which

---

[60] Homer A. Kent, Jr., *Ephesians: The Glory of the Church*, Everyman's Bible Commentary (Chicago: Moody Press, 1971), 29.

they should pray."[61] This is for everyone to have, no matter a person's IQ or aptitude.

It always amazes me to see those in the body of Christ without much of an educational background who, by the Spirit's enablement, grasp spiritual truths way beyond those with higher credentials. The psalmist spoke of this idea: "I have more understanding than all my teachers, for your testimonies are my meditation" (119:99). No matter where believers find themselves in personal spiritual development, they should pray for and avail themselves of this essential and basic blessing. Pray with the psalmist, "Open my eyes, that I may behold wondrous things out of your law" (v. 18).

Gaining Greater Convictions

Another reason to see this prayer for the Ephesian believers as important is because Paul prayed the exact same thing for the Colossian believers:

Col. 1:9–10 *And so, from the day we heard, we have not ceased to pray for you, asking that you may be filled with the knowledge of his will in all spiritual wisdom and understanding, so as to walk in a manner worthy of the Lord, fully pleasing to him, bearing fruit in every good work and increasing in the knowledge of God.*

Whether Paul was praying for the Colossian or Ephesian church, he expected these Christians to be able to gain greater levels of spiritual wisdom and revelation. Why? Because of their prior illumination or enlightenment by the Holy Spirit at their salvation (see Eph. 1:18).

What does this greater level of illumination really look like? Again, this is not new revelation but a greater conviction of what has already been revealed to believers. In Ephesians 1, Paul called this "revelation in the knowledge of him" (v. 17); this is simply knowledge sourced in God. He detailed specifically what he meant in the following verses. With laser precision, he pinpointed what he wanted them to know. He said, "… that you may know what is the hope to which he has called you, what are the riches of his glorious inheritance in the saints, and what is the immeasurable greatness of his power toward us who believe, according to the working of his great might …" (vv. 18b–19).

---

[61] Charles Hodge, *Ephesians*, The Geneva Series of Commentaries (Carlisle, PA: Banner of Truth, 1856; 1991,), 41.

Three Convictions

Here, he listed three spiritual convictions that they were to gain. See them as three categories: salvation's guarantee, salvation's indescribable wealth, and salvation's inexhaustible power.

Salvation's Guarantee

First is salvation's guarantee. In verse 18, Paul expressed his desire that the Ephesians "… know what is the hope to which he has called [them]." Whenever the word "hope" is used in the context of salvation, it is not talking about wishful thinking but a done deal or settled reality. To be "called" essentially means to be summoned by God to salvation by his effectual call. Consequently, this is not simply talking about evangelism, where an appeal is made to someone to believe. This is about God irresistibly drawing a person to saving faith. So here Paul was praying for them to simply come to grips with the reality of a guaranteed place in heaven.

For believers to know they are going to heaven produces a deep, settling effect that is essential for being a productive servant of the Lord. Sadly, believers who constantly waver in assurance of salvation often end up wasting time, focusing on themselves instead of others who are needing encouragement or are needing to hear the gospel.

Salvation's Inexhaustible Wealth

In the second part of verse 18, Paul moved from the believer's hope of heaven to the possession that is in heaven. He described salvation's indescribable wealth, calling it "… the riches of his glorious inheritance in the saints." There are many symbolic pictures given in Scripture that indicate what believers will have in heaven—terms like "crowns," "streets of gold," or being "co-heirs who will reign with Christ." But here Paul was not calling believers to simply count their heavenly money this side of eternity; rather, he was longing for these believers to grasp that, in God, they had everything! They had indescribable wealth in light of the fact that everything glorious awaited them in heaven—guaranteed (see Matt. 13:46; 1 Pet. 1:4). Believers now and forever can know they are rich toward God (see Luke 12:21).

Salvation's Inexhaustible Power

Lastly, Paul wanted them to gain the conviction that they had an incredible resource in the Lord. In verse 19, he described the believer's access to the Lord's inexhaustible power. He wanted them to know "... what is the immeasurable greatness of his power toward us who believe, according to the working of his great might." He heaped six descriptive terms, one on top of the other, to describe this immense power of God. Each word overlaps the other, creating a cumulative picture of God's exceeding power and strength. The first three words are found in the phrase "immeasurable greatness of his power." This combination of terms conveys the idea of something that is beyond possible in understanding. Trying to understand God's power is like trying to follow a ballistic missile that has been launched. God's power surpasses, or exceeds, all greatness in terms of size. It is more than any and all other forms of power.

The last three descriptive terms regarding this power are found in the phrase "... according to the working of his great might." Paul painted a glorious picture of what this church had—and all Christians have—access to. He showed the power as operative, energized, and strong. When he depicted this power as being "according to ... his great might," he uniquely connected what believers have to its source—God himself. In essence, the nature of this power is aligned with the very nature of God. This is enemy-crushing, tide-turning power, like that of a victorious king over an enemy in battle. God is mighty, ensuring that his power will accomplish all his objectives. There is no better example regarding the power Christians have from God than the one he chooses: that this power is the same that resurrected and enthroned Jesus at the Father's right-hand, over-all creation, and over God's beloved church (Eph. 1:20–23).

To be illumined by this power is to see these concepts as concretely as if seeing "... a bulldozer [having] the ability, capacity, and potential of routing out trees. By looking at it, one senses its inherent strength but when its engine roars and it begins to move, its power of mastery becomes obvious."[62] Paul's logic here was simple: because they were saved, they were illumined. And because they had been illumined, they needed to grasp these three key concepts—salvation's guarantee, wealth, and power. To truly be illumined to know these truths is extraordinary.

ILLUMINED IN SPIRITUAL REALITIES

The idea that Paul was praying for this church to be illumined regarding spiritual realities is threaded throughout Ephesians. Chapter 3 introduces

---

[62] Harold Hoehner, *Ephesians: An Exegetical Commentary* (Grand Rapids: Baker Academic, 2002), 271.

what could be seen as Paul's second prayer, in which he prayed that the Ephesian believers would know the rich love they had received in Christ. In Ephesians 3:16–19, he asked that they would be "strengthened with power through his Spirit in [their] inner being, so that Christ may dwell in [their] hearts through faith," and that they "may have strength to … know the love of Christ that surpasses knowledge, that [they] may be filled with all the fullness of God."

Paul prayed that God, according to his rich glory, would illumine their inner being so that, by faith, they would grasp the deep, deep love of Jesus. In verse 19, Paul said that this love "surpasses knowledge." He was readily admitting that, from a strictly human or superficial standpoint, the Ephesians would not be able to understand this love; grasping this kind of divine love in this way, at this level, necessitates the work of the Spirit. This is beyond mere human thinking—it necessitates illumined thinking.

Filled with All the Fullness of God

What is interesting to note is how Paul characterized this work of God as being "filled with all the fullness of God." Paul used "fullness" throughout the book of Ephesians, each time in reference to a spiritual dimension. In 1:23, Jesus, as the head of the church, was said to be "the fullness of him who fills all in all," the life-giving source as the head over his body. As we have seen, 3:19 was Paul's prayer for believers to be spiritually "filled with all the fullness of God." Paul later addressed this again, commanding believers to "be filled with the Spirit" (5:18).

The context of the book sheds light on this command. In 4:1, Paul exhorted the believers in their daily Christian living, calling them to "walk in a manner worthy of [their] calling." The idea here was that this church could fall prey to the influences that surrounded them in the worldly society of Ephesus. Immorality and idol worship were two main components of the city's reputation, and Paul's concern was for the Ephesians' holiness—that they not slip back into former sinful habits that characterized their lives prior to their becoming believers.

In 5:17–18, Paul challenged them to flee their former party lifestyles and instead to pursue God's will. Specifically, he said that, instead of being "foolish," they needed to "understand what the will of the Lord is" (v. 17); he then restated this in saying, "do not get drunk with wine … but be filled with the Spirit" (v. 18). There are many interpretations of what it means for a believer to "be filled with the Spirit," but one key pointer must be that Paul again used the word "filled." Both of Paul's prayers in this letter (1:15–23 and 3:14–21) were for these believers to be illumined, to know or understand spiritual truths, and the commands in 5:17–18 should be understood as the church's way to respond.

Submitting to Biblical Convictions

Though illumination is the Spirit's work in the heart of a believer, this command shows that believers are still responsible to yield themselves to this work. In fact, in 5:17–18, three of the four commands are in the passive voice: "do not be foolish," "do not get drunk," and "be filled with the Spirit" (the Greek literally says, "be filled in Spirit"). This points to the atmosphere of the believer's thinking, emphasizing the necessity for believers to yield themselves to the Spirit's work in their lives. In verse 17, Paul calls them to actively "understand" God's will for holiness, and then calls them to submit their hearts to the act of being "filled with the Spirit" (v. 18). This filling can be understood as the believer yielding him or herself to the Spirit's work of illumination (compare Ps. 119:18).

In Philippians 1:9, Paul similarly prayed that the love of the church in Philippi would "… abound more and more, with knowledge and all discernment"; again, in Colossians 1:9, he prayed that the church in Colossae would "… be filled with the knowledge of his will in all spiritual wisdom and understanding." This was an often-repeated desire Paul had for the church at large. As in Ephesians, Paul's prayer for the Colossians took on a practical dimension in chapter 3. Having prayed for this church to gain "knowledge" and "spiritual wisdom"—again, synonymous with the work of illumination— Paul put legs on this request, exhorting believers to actively "seek the things that are above, where Christ is …" (v. 1) and then to "Let the word of Christ dwell in [them] richly" (v. 16). Both commands emphasize the role believers are to take in being illumined. Paul directed believers to focus their minds on biblical content—here, "the word of Christ." As with the Ephesians, believers were illumined for the express purpose of gaining spiritual convictions, which came when the Spirit impressed the truths of God's Word in greater depth, creating greater certainty.

Established in Christ–Like Convictions

The Apostle Peter, like Paul, emphasized a great confidence in the Word as the agent by which a person is illumined. Peter wrote some of the clearest teaching in all the New Testament on this subject in 2 Peter 1. Sensing that the end of his life was drawing near (v. 14), Peter wanted the churches in his charge to be secure. Although he recognized that these Christians were "established in the truth" (v. 12), he made no apologies about restating what they knew, "by way of reminder" (v. 13), so that they would be able to recall it after he was gone (v. 15). What he said was comprised of two parts: Peter first recounted his experience with Christ on the Mount of Transfiguration (see Matt. 17:1–8), then he gave a higher endorsement for the Word of God. He wrote:

2 Pet. 1:16–21 *For we did not follow cleverly devised myths when we made known to you the power and coming of our Lord Jesus Christ, but we were eyewitnesses of his majesty. For when he received honor and glory from God the Father, and the voice was borne to him by the Majestic Glory, "This is my beloved Son, with whom I am well pleased," we ourselves heard this very voice borne from heaven, for we were with him on the holy mountain. And we have the prophetic word more fully confirmed, to which you will do well to pay attention as to a lamp shining in a dark place, until the day dawns and the morning star rises in your hearts, knowing this first of all, that no prophecy of Scripture comes from someone's own interpretation. For no prophecy was ever produced by the will of man, but men spoke from God as they were carried along by the Holy Spirit.*

Peter recounted the experience he, James, and John had when they saw the glory and power of Christ firsthand, which was followed by hearing God the Father's voice of affirmation. This was an unparalleled experience. However, instead of holding this experience up as his authority, in verse 19, he wrote of something "more fully confirmed" than this incredible experience: "the prophetic word."

Peter testified to having heard directly from God but affirmed a higher testimony—"the prophetic word more fully confirmed," illumined to each and every believer's heart by the Spirit. He esteemed the objective revelation of the Word of God above the experiential revelation of the transfigured Christ. Peter was making the point that, barring Christ's return in their lifetime, his readers would never see Christ's glory in that way, yet they were still on solid ground. Their certainty came from their confidence in the Word that had been illumined to their hearts. Peter likened illumination to "… a lamp shining in a dark place" and the dawning of the day when "… the morning star rises in [believers'] hearts" (v. 19).

This experience of illumination resonates with every believer. Peter elevated Scripture above experience as the means for knowing God. This means that the same illumination he had can be had by all believers—even those of us who will not see the risen Christ until we arrive in heaven. Peter brought everything back to Scripture and reminds us that Scripture originated from the Holy Spirit (v. 21). As a fitting conclusion to his epistle, he wrote to the end that these believers would mature in their spiritual convictions, exhorting them to "… grow in the grace and knowledge of our Lord and Savior Jesus Christ" (3:18).

Convictions That Give Assurance of Your Salvation

The last author we will examine here is the Apostle John. The son of Zebedee referred to the necessity of illumination in protecting believers from heretical teaching. John, like Peter, was advanced in years and coming to the end of his ministry as he wrote the book of 1 John. Over and over again, he referred to those under his shepherding care as "my little children" (see, for example, 1 John 2:1). Out of a desire to guard and protect his flock, he warned them of the false teachers, those in the church whom he called "antichrists" (v. 18). They were those who denied "that Jesus is the Christ," ultimately denying "the Father and the Son" (v. 22). John affirmed that the believers whom he shepherded and loved had "been anointed … and [had] knowledge," so they were able to combat these heresies (v. 20).

The concept of being anointed comes directly from the Old Testament priesthood. Anointing was a symbolic ceremony whereby priests were set apart from the rest of Israel as those who would carry out an intercessory ministry between the nation and God. The primary example of this was the Aaronic priesthood, in which men were designated to perform the ceremonial duties (Exod. 30:30). In Old Testament history, Israel's kings were also anointed (1 Sam. 16:12), symbolizing their significant role as those separated by God to act as his spokesmen, intercessors, and mediators as they ruled God's nation. To be anointed meant being covered with oil. This conveyed that the anointed person was owned by the LORD and was consecrated for the LORD's use. As we saw earlier, Christ quoted Isaiah 61:1, saying of himself, "The Spirit of the Lord is upon me, because he has anointed me to proclaim good news to the poor" (Luke 4:18). Jesus was not referring here to a physical anointing, but to the Spirit's illuminating work to empower him "to proclaim" the gospel.

By understanding the foundation of the ceremony of anointing from the Old Testament, it becomes clearer what John meant in 1 John as he expanded this picture to a spiritual anointing for all believers. This anointing, instead of covering the outer skin, is dealing with the inner man. John wrote in 2:20–21 of believers in the church, "But you have been anointed by the Holy One, and you all have knowledge. I write to you, not because you do not know the truth, but because you know it, and because no lie is of the truth." Note that the anointing is connected with "knowledge" (v. 20) and that the believers "know it" (v. 21). As with the Old Testament symbol, believers are set apart, but now it is their minds that are set apart—to the truth.

This goes back to our main point. John affirmed that believers have illumined spiritual convictions, what he called "knowledge" (v. 20). For those to whom he wrote, and for all believers, these convictions serve to protect against false teachers and false teaching. Believers are not solely dependent upon spiritually gifted teachers in the church to interpret the meaning of Scripture (v. 27). Though gifted teachers are part of what makes a church strong, edified and protected (1 Cor. 12:28; Eph. 4:11; 1 Tim. 3:2), it is the anointing of the Spirit of God that is the guide to truth. This anointing can and should be likened to the burning convictions that were born in the two disciples on the road to Emmaus.

9
Conclusion

Without a biblical gauge, there is no credible way in which to evaluate whether or not preaching is making an authentic difference for the glory of God. It is important to have biblical expectations from a biblical framework in order to understand the effect the Word is to have as it is preached. I have presented these four categories in the hope that they will build just such a grid to shape the expectations for preachers and for hearers.

It is typical that a preacher today does not think biblically about how to evaluate his preaching ministry. Too often, an extra-biblical measuring stick, such as "attendance" or "offerings," is used to gauge success. This can lead to preachers becoming performance-based in the pulpit, all because the Holy Spirit's promised ministry of illumination is undervalued or simply forgotten. Illumination is missing in preaching because it is missing in the preacher. When the Holy Spirit's role is divorced from personal study, this naturally affects the pulpit, and thus the hearers.

Sometimes, a preacher looks for the Holy Spirit to come and bless his speaking ability apart from blessing the Word as it is proclaimed. What happens when this extra blessing of the Spirit does not appear? The preacher may become confused and discouraged. This kind of subjective evaluation of preaching leaves out the Spirit's role of illumining the preached Word. Regrettably, many books on the Holy Spirit reinforce this kind of subjectivity by completely skipping over the theme of illumination as it pertains to the pastor's study and pulpit. Again, the clear concern is a lack of biblical expectations for both preachers and preaching, for the private study and public ministry.

Regardless of a preacher's platform or phase of ministry, confidence in communicating rises or falls based on the expectation of what preaching will accomplish. A clear understanding of illumination will, like a fresh breeze, offer a renewed sense of confidence in disciplined exegetical study coupled with energetic, affectionate, and expositional preaching. It will change the preacher. This God-inspired and God-blessed work of illumination can turn study into worship. No longer is study mere preparation to speak, it is worship of Jesus. Understood and prioritized correctly, preaching becomes the overflow of what has first happened in the preacher's heart and mind. This kind of preaching connects the ministry of the Spirit with the Word of God, reinvigorating both study and pulpit.

There is such a noteworthy difference in sermon preparation when it is approached with biblical expectations in mind, and the four categories we have outlined can become a framework for developing right biblical expectations. They can prompt many questions, such as: "What is going to happen when I preach?"; "Is the Holy Spirit stirring my affections while I study, pray, and meditate?"; "Will the Lord save somebody from hell when I preach this time?"; "Will someone become angry or bitter and reject what I am going to say?"; "Will someone's spiritual life be refreshed as he or she takes another spiritual step toward being like Jesus?" Questions like these reflect a heart that is beginning to understand the dynamic of illumination in preparation, preaching, and hearing.

FOUR CATEGORIES OF ILLUMINATION

An example from the Apostle Paul's preaching ministry may be the best way to illustrate these biblical expectations. This episode contains the four categories of illumination we have outlined, linking a right view of illumination with a right view of preaching. In Acts 17, Paul, having taught the resurrection of Jesus in the synagogues in Athens, was compelled by Epicurean and Stoic philosophers to take this message to a different forum: Mars Hill. He took a different approach with this audience as he preached the resurrection of Jesus and called those listening to repent (vv. 30–31). See the various ways in which those present responded: "Now when they heard of the resurrection of the dead, some mocked. But others said, 'We will hear you again about this.' So Paul went out from their midst. But some men joined him and believed, among whom also were Dionysius the Areopagite and a woman named Damaris and others with them" (vv. 32–34).

Here, the four categories of illumination can be seen. **First**, based on Paul's communication of the Word, **people responded**. The way God designed for these hearers to be challenged was through preaching. Paul gave an impassioned delivery, saying, "What therefore you worship as unknown, this I proclaim to you" (v. 23).

Second, the preaching of the Word brought some under condemnation. There were those who overtly rejected the gospel—"**some mocked**." People who make fun of the Word of God are in a very sobering and dangerous place. They are not unlike the crowds who mocked Jesus while he was dying on the cross and who, at the end, will be found scoffing and mocking Jesus's return (2 Pet. 3:3–4). These ungodly ones will be destroyed by the very Lord they mock (v. 7).

Third, some were illumined and some, saying "**We will hear you again**," were what Owen called "pre-illumined."[63] Though still unregenerate, these are people Jesus might have characterized as he did a certain scribe, saying, "You are not far from the kingdom of God" (Mark 12:34). Those who were asking for more teaching can be placed along with those who "joined [Paul] and believed" under the category of conversion. They were seeking the light, and were on the cusp of regeneration, which is where illumination begins.

Fourth, the words "**joined and believed**" can be read as a strong confirmation of these men and this woman—assuming, for the sake of this work, that those who joined Paul as committed followers would be gaining convictions as they grew in grace and in the knowledge of Jesus and his Word (see 2 Pet. 3:18).

Preparing Your message for Clarity

With these biblical expectations in mind, how ought the preacher approach preaching? While there is no exact formula to ensure Spirit-illumined preaching, there are two clear steps that a preacher must take while he prepares his text for clarity.

First, the preacher must **pray** for God's Spirit to illumine his mind in the study, just as the psalmist prayed (Ps. 119:18), and the Apostle Paul prayed for believers to be illumined (see Chapter 6: Convictions through Illumination). Here, the communicator realizes his absolute need for the Spirit's intervention as he casts himself upon God in complete reliance. Here is an example of this prayer in study: "Lord, please make the Scripture clear

---

[63] Owen, *The Holy Spirit*, 135–38.

to me so I can present the truth in an understandable way, so that people will come away spiritually awakened and affected by it."

Second, the preacher must **meditate**. He must move beyond academics to a deep consideration of his biblical passage: what it meant when it was originally written, what it means for his own life personally, and, finally, what it means for his people. Meditation is the time when the Spirit of God grabs a heart with his Word—convincing the believer of the text's veracity and convicting of sin. Meditation should result in a preacher gaining convictions and deep abiding affections over the profound significance of the text to be preached. Once illumined, the preacher's role is to convey those truths to his hearers while maintaining a deep reliance upon the text he is preaching; he does this in the hope that the Spirit of God will likewise illumine the hearts of his hearers through the agency of the Word preached, creating deep convictions, spiritual growth, and greater depth and height of worship.

Study for Clarity

Instead of relying on academic minutiae, contrived mystical effects, pragmatic manipulations, or even homiletical abilities, the preacher must see the need for the Holy Spirit to sweep him up as he pores over his text each week in heartfelt prayer and meditation, with the hope that those who listen will consequently be swept up as well. Though there may come seasons of dryness in study and preaching, this study of illumination clearly reveals that boldness in preaching is generated from convictions impressed on a heart that has been illumined from texts studied, and that these Spirit-wrought biblical convictions translate into empowered, impassioned, and ignited sermons.

The preacher should never exchange the time and discipline necessary for exegetical study for time spent in prayer and meditation but must make a way for both of these elements. John Owen, who contributed what may be the essential theological treatment of the doctrine of illumination, documented this crucial harmony of disciplines: "... the means of the right interpretation of the Scripture, and understanding the mind of God therein, are of two sorts,—first, such as prescribed unto us in a way of duty, as prayer, meditation on the word itself, and the like; and, secondly, disciplinary, in the accommodation of arts and sciences, with all kind of learning, unto that work …"[64]

Owen's words reiterate that the reason why the preacher must carefully exegete his passage is to clearly understand it and, in turn, to accurately present it (see 2 Tim. 2:15). Once clarity is gained through prayer and disciplined study, the preacher can effectively and easily ponder his text, meditating so as to be gripped by the implications of it as he is illumined by God's Spirit. Bible scholar Dr. Bernard L. Ramm depicts this very clearly in two illustrations borrowed from Danish philosopher and existentialist Søren Kierkegaard:

> Kierkegaard poses the question how a lover reads a love letter from his lover when they happen to speak two different languages. The first thing the lover must do with the letter is to translate it. He gets out his dictionary of the foreign language—perhaps even a grammar—and goes to work. He translates it word by word, line by line, paragraph by paragraph, until the entire translated letter is on the desk before him.

> But doing all that hard work of translating that letter into his language is not to read the letter as a love letter. Now that he has the complete translation he relaxes, leans back in his chair, and reads the translated letter as a love letter.

> So it is with the Holy Scripture. We cannot avoid all the hard work of looking up Hebrew and Greek words, puzzling over constructions, consulting commentaries, and other such helps. But doing this careful academic job of translating and interpreting Scripture is not to read the Word of God as the Word of God…. But to read the Scripture as the Word of God he must read it the second time. Now it is no longer an academic task but it is a case of letting God's Word get through to a man's soul as God's Word. It is in the second reading of the letter that the Holy Spirit … enters into the process of understanding Holy Scripture.

Kierkegaard gives a second illustration:

> A little boy is to be spanked by his father. While the father goes for the rod the boy stuffs the bottom of his pants with several table napkins.

---

[64] John Owen, William H. Goold, ed., *The Works of John Owen*, vol. iv (London: Banner of Truth, 1850; 1967), 126.

When the father returns and administers the whipping the boys feels no pain as the napkins absorb the whack of the rod. The little boy represents the biblical scholars. They pad their britches with their lexicons, commentaries, and concordances. As a result the Scripture never reaches them as the Word of God. Having nullified its power by shielding themselves with their academic paraphernalia, they thus never hear the Scriptures as the Word of God. If they would unpack their books from their britches (which are necessary rightfully used, as illustrated in the story of the love letter) then the Scriptures could get through to them as the Word of God. Allowing Holy Scripture to get through to us as the Word of God is the special work of the Holy Spirit.[65]

Preach It Because You Believe It!

Moving from expectations for study, what kind of expectations ought the preacher to have for illumination in preaching? The Apostle Paul stands out as a superb example. His testimony as a preacher to the Thessalonians was simple. He reminded them in no uncertain terms that "... our gospel came to you not only in word, but also in power and in the Holy Spirit and with full conviction. You know what kind of men we proved to be among you for your sake" (1 Thess. 1:5). Paul's preaching was authentic. Why? Because it was the Word of God empowered by the Spirit of God, and it burst from his illumined heart "with full conviction!" Illumination starts in the study, but the Spirit's role of illumining the heart is also necessary in the pulpit. The preacher stands as a humble vessel ready for God's Word to pour from his mouth, and the deep impressions of the truths studied are pressed even deeper into his heart as he declares them. Like Paul, he simply believes and so speaks (see the chapter on Conviction and 2 Cor. 4:13). This dynamic is what makes preaching unique and powerful. Being illumined while preaching is how illumined convictions are passed from the communicator to the listener as they hear with spiritual ears. Owen explained the crucial reason why the preacher must seek to be illumined:

> And there is not any truth of greater importance for men to be established in; for unless they have a full assurance of understanding in themselves, unless they hold their persuasion of the sense of Scripture revelations from God alone, if their spiritual judgment of truth and falsehood depend on the authority of men, they will never be able to

---

[65] Ramm, *Rapping about the Spirit*, 85–86. See Søren Kierkegaard, and Howard V. Hong and Edna H. Hong, trs. and eds., *For Self-Examination in Kierkegaard's Writings*, vol. xxi (Princeton: Princeton University Press, 1851; 1990), 26–35.

undergo any suffering for the truth or to perform any duty unto God in a right manner.[66]

This "inward persuasion of the Holy Spirit" is what gave martyrs of old strength to give their lives for the gospel.[67] This blood earnestness should be no different for the preacher in the pulpit. Illumined preaching flows from the illumined preacher—the preacher who is convinced that the stakes of pastoral duty are eternal; this man preaches a message he is willing to die for.

Preach for an Audience of One

And what of the hearers? What ought the preacher to expect of them? The preacher who is ministering with wrong expectations can be emotionally tossed up and down as if in a turbulent sea by his perceived successes and failures in preaching. Right biblical expectations will not only inform but hopefully also resuscitate discouraged preachers. The Spirit's promised ministry has been there all along. Some will hear and have hearts illumined by the Spirit to believe, understand, and grow in spiritual convictions. Others will hear, reject, and remain under condemnation. The preacher must expect that, whatever the outcome, whatever God's purpose, God will be glorified.

Let us make this more personal, and hopefully very practical. What does this mean for us and our preaching ministries? What should we expect when we preach? As Spirit-filled preachers, we should assume that the Lord will illumine our minds both in the study and during the preaching event. Listen to the way Carl Hargrove described this balance in his thesis on the Spirit's role in preaching:

> It is … a reasonable, if not a necessary conclusion, that the Spirit does illumine the mind in preaching, since He does in the interpretive process. Illuminational preaching is that which depends on the Spirit to take the effort of exegesis and, according to the Spirit's sovereign plan, make those thoughts cogent in the mind of the preacher—he experiences what the Psalmist longed to experience [see Ps. 119:18, 25, 27, and 31], yet in a different context—the preaching event. It would include insight that is beyond the preacher's normal giftedness and abilities, and a freedom to express these thoughts in a manner that is

---

[66] Owen, *Works*, 123.
[67] Calvin, *Institutes*, 92.

most edifying to his listeners. Illuminational preaching includes bringing the truth of Scripture to bear in the minds of the audience.[68]

Also, the apostles who were commissioned by Christ to preach likewise anticipated the promise that they would be Spirit-illumined after Jesus was gone. In this way, the apostles served as forerunners for all illumined preaching, since their ministry was obviously very similar to and yet very different from that of today's preacher. Hargrove clarifies the distinctions:

> What the apostles experienced was both illuminational and revelational—their minds were enlightened to remember truths of the Scriptures and the ministry of Christ as promised by the Lord (John 14:26) and therefore they were channels for revelation, which would be moved from oral to written record. For post-apostolic preaching, the mind of the minister is still and only illumined to the truths of Scripture, and the mind of the listener is illumined to the truth of the message.[69]

This being the case, we ought to expect, within our minds, an illumined dynamic whereby we gain more and more conviction and affection over the text during delivery. Dr. Albert Mohler affirmed this, recognizing that preachers are instruments who "speak what [God] Himself has spoken … through the preaching of Scripture under the illumination and testimonium of the Holy Spirit."[70]

What of our hearers? Knowing that it is ultimately the Lord who gives life or death (conversion or condemnation) as we preach might tempt us to take a passive attitude. This would be unbiblical and lacking the integrity demanded by our calling. D. Martyn Lloyd-Jones says,

> Do you expect anything to happen when you get up to preach in a pulpit? Or do you just say to yourself, "Well, I have prepared my address, I am going to give them this address; some of them will appreciate it and some will not?" Are you expecting it to be the turning

---

[68] Carl A. Hargrove, "The Role of the Holy Spirit as Convictor and Supporter in Preaching," (ThM Thesis, The Master's Seminary, 2006), 115.

[69] Ibid., 114.

[70] Albert Mohler, "Why Do We Preach? A Foundation for Christian Preaching, Part One," December 15, 2005, "Commentary," at: AlbertMohler.com.

point in someone's life? Are you expecting anyone to have a climactic experience? That is what preaching is meant to do.[71]

In the mystery of God, instead of being passive or blasé, we are called to see ourselves as a means by which the Lord brings eternal life (1 Tim. 4:16).

Preach to the Glory of Christ

With this in mind, let us expect nothing less of ourselves than to prepare and deliver clear, authentic, enlivened, heart-affected truth with people's souls in view. Let us expect that some will gain deeper and higher Spirit-given convictions as they hear God's Spirit-inspired text. At the same time, expect that some will hear the Word of God and reject it as foolishness, only to continue as blind men and women down a path toward condemnation. Understanding this balance may keep us from spiritual pride and a "holier-than-thou" attitude. As Paul said, "For we are the aroma of Christ to God among those who are being saved and among those who are perishing, to one a fragrance from death to death, to the other a fragrance from life to life. Who is sufficient for these things?" (2 Cor. 2:15–16).

Paul's attitude toward his preaching was anything but resigned or passive. He felt the highs and lows, and he had a real grip on the eternal stakes of his ministry—that people either gained life or were condemned. He was God-centered. He knew he was an instrument and only that; he was God's vessel for pouring out his Word on people. Paul was no different from preachers who have gone before or after him. Whether we look at the prophets or the Son of God himself, the results of illumined preaching are the same. Whether we evaluate Calvin, Luther, Owen, or Edwards, the results of illumined preaching are the same. Why should we expect anything different? The blind will see, the deaf will hear, and some will reject.

So, what is our admonition? Preach the Word—but only after having first been illumined by it. Then, with a clear conscience, preach, expecting those listening to gain convictions, illumined convictions, the Bible's convictions. This is authentic biblical communication. We preach as messengers, shepherds, and soldiers, ever persevering in our calling and duty, with the knowledge that people will both accept and reject the Word of God. The Bible sets this agenda—it is our acid test for how we are doing. This is what

---

[71] D. Martyn Lloyd-Jones, *Preaching and Preachers* (London: Hodder and Stoughton, 1971; 1985), 325.

makes our backbones strong and our confidence sure in what the Holy Spirit will accomplish through his truth proclaimed. This blessed ministry of the Spirit "… may rightly be called the key that unlocks for us the treasures of the Kingdom of Heaven [see Rev. 3:7]; and his illumination, the keenness of our insight."[72]

---

[72] Calvin, *Institutes*, 542.

10
Appendix I
The Historical Context for a Biblical Theology of Illumination

Throughout church history, men of God have recognized the significance of this doctrine that is so widely found throughout the Word. The specific significance that this doctrine exemplifies is its role in protecting the message of the gospel. An examination of theologians throughout church history testifies to this doctrine's powerful ability to illumine the truth of God's Word.

REFORMING ILLUMINATION

Understanding the reality and importance of illumination drove the church in the early 16th century to value the expository preaching of men such as Martin Luther, John Calvin, and William Tyndale. Puritan writers like John Owen and others were profoundly influenced by the doctrine of illumination, as evidenced by the way it flows in and through their writings and reflections.[73] Jonathan Edwards, the great American preacher and theologian from the 18th century, was another man of God whose writings and thoughts were permeated with this doctrine. It has been said that for one to truly understand Edwards' apologetics, sermons, and teachings, one must first grasp

---

[73] Stephen J. Nichols, *An Absolute Sort of Certainty: The Holy Spirit and the Apologetics of Jonathan Edwards* (Phillipsburg, NJ: P & R, 2003), 47.

his understanding of the doctrine of illumination.[74] Follow along as we retrace those who lifted the doctrine of illumination from the pages of Scripture and imprinted it on the hearts and souls of their hearers.

John Calvin

The man who stands out as a forerunner in crystallizing the teaching of illumination is John Calvin. Reading his testimony, it is readily apparent that this doctrine meant a great deal to him. When Calvin was a young man in the early 1500s, a significant transition was taking place across Europe. Throughout the Middle Ages, God's Word had been held at a distance from the common man by the established church, resulting in massive spiritual darkness in the world. Most people did not have access to God's Word because it was not translated into the common tongue. The Bible was unreadable and impossible to understand; however, with the Protestant Reformation, all this changed. Access to the Bible was gained. In fact, one of the heart-cries of the Protestant Reformation was the slogan *post tenebras lux*: "After darkness, light." This light was the spiritual light of illumination believers receive from God's Word. At this point in history, through the Word being preached and read, spiritual awakening came with blinding brilliance and spread the gospel across the globe.

Calvin understood well the need for people to be illumined, so from the very start of his ministry in Geneva, he was committed to expository preaching, as was reflected in his work ethic. He was a busy pastor. His time was filled with counseling, visiting sick members, writing letters, officiating at public ceremonies such as weddings, baptisms, and the Lord's Table, as well as with the private duty of praying for his flock. He was, however, first and foremost a preacher. He devoted much of his time to studying his Bible, preparing to preach two sermons every Sunday plus one sermon every day of the week on alternating weeks. Every two weeks, Calvin was preaching, on average, nine to ten times. He also taught as a theological professor and preached to and mentored local Genevan pastors on Fridays. So, in a typical year, Calvin preached about 286 sermons.[75] It has been said that his elders insisted upon this rigorous preaching program so that the light from his preaching would effect change in the surrounding Genevan culture.[76] While this arduous preaching schedule must have been physically demanding, his

---

[74] Ibid.
[75] David L. Larsen, *The Company of Preachers: A History of Biblical Preaching from the Old Testament to the Modern* Era (Grand Rapids: Kregel, 1998), 167.
[76] Walter Kaiser, "The Power of the Word of God," sermon preached at The Bible Church of Little Rock, October 22, 2006, at: http://64.19.50.210/Default.aspx.

elders gave good counsel. The light from his pulpit ministry is still shining around the world today.

For Calvin, this was not an unwelcome requirement because he understood the doctrine of illumination well. Throughout his *Institutes* and sermons runs the teaching of what he called "the internal testimony of the Holy Spirit," which is the certainty of the Scripture confirmed by the Spirit in the heart of the believer. Calvin also called this "the internal witness of the Spirit" or the "enlightenment" that comes through "the medium of verbal testimony [where a believer's] blind eyes of the spirit are opened, and divine realities come to be recognized and embraced for what they are."[77]

He was so convinced of the reality of the "inward persuasion of the Holy Spirit"[78] that he compared it to his physical experience, saying illumination was "... as immediate and unanalysable as the perceiving of a color, or a taste, by physical sense ... [that] when it happened [a person knew] ... it had happened."[79] Calvin clearly stated that the testimonium, or this witness of the Spirit, was not some kind of additional revelation beyond the Scripture. He says, "Therefore the Spirit, promised to us, has not the task of inventing new and unheard-of revelations, or of forging a new kind of doctrine, to lead us away from the received doctrine of the gospel, but of sealing our minds [the testimonium] with that very doctrine which is commended by the gospel."[80]

The Spirit's work "... awakens us, as from the dead, to see and taste the divine reality of God in Scripture, which authenticates it as God's own word."[81] Again, for Calvin, the Word of God is saving, but is made certain by the "inward persuasion of the Holy Spirit."[82] So a person illumined will automatically have the perspective that Scripture "wins reverence for itself by its own majesty ... illumined by its power, we believe ...; but above human judgment we affirm with utter certainty (just as if we were gazing upon the majesty of God himself) that it has flowed to us from the very mouth of God

---

[77] J. I. Packer, "Calvin the Theologian," in G. E. Duffield, ed., *John Calvin: A Collection of Essays* (London: Sutton Courtenay Press, 1966), 166.
[78] Calvin, *Institutes*, 80.
[79] Packer, "Calvin the Theologian," 166.
[80] Calvin, *Institutes*, 94.
[81] Packer, "Calvin the Theologian," 166.
[82] Ibid., 92.

..."[83] Calvin declared this as "more excellent than reason," when, by the sealing work of the Spirit, the Bible obtains full "acceptance" in a person's heart.[84]

Reading Calvin's testimony of his conversion makes it easy to understand why this doctrine meant so much to him. For Calvin, this teaching framed his personal experience of becoming a Christian. While the exact date of his conversion is not known, some time after 1533 Calvin described his own original illumination that took place while he was still a practicing Catholic. What is noteworthy is how he measured the authenticity of his conversion in terms of the spiritual light that caused his mind and affections to be moved by the Word. Calvin describes this thus:

> ... A very different form of doctrine started up, not one which led us away from the Christian profession, but one which brought it back to its fountain ... to its original purity. Offended by the novelty, I lent an unwilling ear, and at first, I confess, strenuously and passionately resisted ... to confess that I had all my life long been in ignorance and error ... I at length perceived, as if light had broken in upon me, in what a sty of error I had wallowed, and how much pollution and impurity I had thereby contracted. Being exceedingly alarmed at the misery into which I had fallen ... as in duty bound, [I] made it my first business to betake myself to thy way [O God], condemning my past life, not without groans and tears. God, by a sudden conversion subdued and brought my mind to a teachable frame.... Having thus received some taste and knowledge of true godliness, I was immediately inflamed with [an] intense desire to make progress.[85]

He was given spiritual eyesight, and he suddenly embraced the truth for what it was—the revelation of God. He had discovered the certainty of Scripture by what he called "the secret testimony of the Spirit" or "the inward persuasion of the Holy Spirit." It is no overstatement to say that his understanding of this doctrine was what drove his ministry in the Word. Why else would John Calvin have given his life to expository preaching? Calvin knew that God's light only shines in a person's soul through the vehicle of biblical truth, and so he devoted his entire life to exegetical study from the Hebrew and Greek Scriptures.[86]

---

[83] Ibid., 80.
[84] Ibid., 79.
[85] Quoted in John Dillenberger, ed., *Introduction, John Calvin: Selections from his Writings* (Scholars Press for the American Academy of Religion, 1975), 26.
[86] Ibid., 14.

History makes it clear that his preaching ministry influenced his own culture, with the effects felt far beyond—reaching even down to today. Calvin maintained the simple commitment to preach truth to his community in Geneva about three out of every four days—all with the purpose of bringing light! What he called the "testimonium" should be categorically understood as an "application" of the general doctrine of illumination.[87] For this reason, Calvin is a foundational theologian for the development of this doctrine as a whole. His commitment to biblical illumination testifies to the doctrine's powerful ability to specify the nature of the gospel message. Calvin is not alone in this historical testimony.

William Tyndale

"W.T. to the Readers", begins the prologue to one of the earliest translations of the New Testament to identify its translator, William Tyndale. Earlier editions of his translation were signed with his full name, but the pressure of being hunted down for committing capital crimes, such as translating the Bible into English, compelled him to be more subtle.[88] What compelled Tyndale to become a fugitive from the law and to forsake his prominent future in scholarship in England?

Two interrelated occasions inspired. First, the shroud of the Roman Catholic Church pitched a dark tent over the people of England so as to keep them blinded from the illuminating truth of the gospel. Second, Tyndale possessed a relentless and uncompromising burden to uncover that dreadful cloak so that even the simplest plowboy would be able to read the Word of truth. Tyndale's zeal for the preaching of God's Word through a reliable and accurate translation of God's Word is captured in a famous debate. Tyndale, engaged in a daring debate with a learned scholar, was met with this appalling statement that, "we are better to be without God's laws than the pope's." To this, Tyndale replied, "I defy the pope and all his laws.... If God spare my life, ere many years I will cause a boy that driveth the plough to know more of the Scripture than thou dost."

Tyndale faced similar opposition and challenges that attempted to hinder the ministry of Martin Luther. Some speculate that these two men may have even crossed paths.[89] Tyndale was fond of Luther's work, as he would

---

[87] J. I. Packer, *God Has Spoken* (Grand Rapids: Baker, 1988), 132.

[88] Steven J. Lawson, *The Daring Mission of William Tyndale*, First ed., A Long Line of Godly Men Profile (Orlando, FL: Reformation Trust, 2015), xix.

[89] Ibid., 11.

often cross-reference his translations from Greek to German with his translations from Greek to English. Just as Luther was interested in providing the German people with the illuminating truth of Scripture, so was Tyndale to the English people.

Tyndale's contribution to the Reformation and to the doctrine of illumination is not the publishing of an impressive library of commentaries. Tyndale's impact was translating the first English New Testament from the Greek and nearly half of the Old Testament from the Hebrew. In the published New Testament translations, Tyndale imprinted another long-lasting mark on Christianity. He prepared extensive prologues that were designed to guide the reader before they read the freshly translated English Bible. In these prologues, Tyndale reveals his own theological convictions which he implored the reader to believe as they read God's Word in their own language. It is remarkable to think that the first English Bible commentaries were infused into the introductory pages of the first translated English Bibles! Within these theological prologues, Tyndale's convictions of illumination shine forth.

In his prologue to the 1525 edition of the English Bible, Tyndale recounts his motivation to defy the government and embark on the daring mission to translate the Bible from the original languages into English. Tyndale explains, "Moreover I supposed it superfluous, for who is so blind tare why light should be shewed to them that walk in darkness, where they cannot but stumble, and where to stumble is the danger of eternal damnation."[90]

Looking back at Tyndale's explanation for his motivation to put on the cloak of a fugitive, we can see another noticeable mark imprinted by Tyndale's writings. The Englishman's motivation manifested from the shroud of tyrannical unbelievers who sought to keep the world from seeing the light of the gospel. They were void of the illuminating light of the gospel because they were in a state of condemnation. A few sentences later, the translator-theologian proclaims that "light destroyeth darkness."[91]

Tyndale ensured that the first translations of the English Bible accurately and reliably communicated God's Word. He knew the importance of putting God's Word into the hands of the people because he knew that those without the light are condemned and that the light saves those who are in darkness. Why? Because Tyndale understood the doctrine of illumination. He

---

[90] William Tyndale, *The Prologue from the Cologne Quarto* (1525).
[91] Ibid.

knew that the Holy Spirit used his Word as the means of granting illumination to the plow boy. Tyndale was motivated to translate the Bible because he understood that in it God speaks to his people and that the light of the gospel proclaimed in the Bible destroys darkness. While Tyndale never used the word "illumination," he understood its principles and the Spirit's work through the Word. May Tyndale, the man of God who gave up his life at the stake for the translation of God's Word into the common tongue, encourage us all to contemplate God's glory through the illuminating work of His Word.

His teachings of condemnation leave a lasting imprint on the doctrine of "condemnation without illumination," and his motivation for translating the Bible in connection with light destroying darkness is the song that this book sings in chapter 5, "Communication for Illumination." While Tyndale has not used these terms, he has set a precedent for these doctrines. Tyndale the man of God, translator-theologian, Reformer, and martyr, has influenced the authors of this book to continue his legacy with the doctrine of illumination.

Reformation on the Horizon

Calvin, Luther, Tyndale, and many other faithful men of the Word lived in an era that was largely void of illumination. After the death, burial, and resurrection of our Lord, the Roman Catholic Church arose, crowning itself as the head of Christ's church and as the authorial interpreter of his Word. The reading of God's Word was forbidden for the commoner, and the interpretation of it was grossly mistreated. God's Word was temporarily covered up as a candle hidden under the basket of the pope and his cronies. Should a passerby attempt to look under that basket at even a glimmer of the beauty of the light that would escape, efforts would be taken to further conceal the light or to persuade the light gazer to move along.

During the Middle Ages, the pope's and his cronies' basket blinded the souls of many. It was for this reason that the Lord raised up men like Calvin, Luther, and Tyndale to flip over the pope's basket and reveal the marvelous light of the gospel. These men bravely confronted a *condemned* world by boldly *communicating* God's Word. They did so because they understood the doctrine of illumination and called sinners to *conversion* in Christ alone through the preaching of the gospel. They taught the word of God, knowing that through illumination, God the Holy Spirit would grant *convictions*. These four—*condemnation, communication, conversion, and conviction*—are the pillars to a biblical theology of illumination. They were foundational to the men who sparked and kindled the Reformation, and they are foundational to every faithful preacher's ministry today.

Not every generation will have need of a Martin Luther nailing ninety-nine theses to the bulletin board of a university. Not every generation will easily identify the need for a Reformation or agree that one has begun. However, every generation does have need faithful men to preach truth in dark times. Some days are darker than others, and Christians can easily be caught in discussion about the darkness when we ought to be about the business of preaching to those in the darkness! Whether the days are shrouded with worldwide pandemics, abuse of governmental authority, or the inevitable persecution of Christ's church, may our thoughts and conversations be about the light that destroyeth darkness! May we be diligent to flip over whoever's basket attempts to conceal that light, and may we have a solid doctrine of illumination which is essential for all days regardless of how dark.

Wrapping It Up

Before concluding this chapter, it will be helpful to clarify as to what I am not saying in this book. I am not suggesting that the Holy Spirit is somehow imprisoned by the Word of God.[92] Rather, I am emphasizing that again and again, I find in Scripture that, in terms of illumination, the same Holy Spirit who inspired the Word (2 Tim. 3:16; 2 Pet. 1:21) "works with the Word (cum verbo) and through the Word (per verbum), not without or apart from the Word (sine verbo)."[93]

On a personal note, my purpose for writing on illumination is more than that I find it fascinating. I want to show that understanding this doctrine is essential to effectively communicate truth. Though the Bible is replete with examples of this teaching, we will journey through just some of the mountain peaks of illumination from the Scripture, surveying them through the lens of our four main categories—condemnation, communication, conversion, and convictions. I would encourage you to read not just as Bible communicators but as simply Christians. Allow the biblical references to prompt your own personal examination. Ask yourself, "Am I in light or darkness?" and "Am I growing closer to Christ as the Spirit opens my eyes to truth?"

---

[92] Hendrikus Berkhof, *The Doctrine of the Holy Spirit: The Annie Kinkead Warfield Lectures, 1963, 1964* (Richmond, VA: John Knox Press, 1964), 38.

[93] R. C. Sproul, "The Internal Testimony of the Holy Spirit," in Norman L. Geisler, ed., *Inerrancy* (Grand Rapids: Zondervan, 1980), 338 (based on the work of G. C. Berkouwer, *Die Heilige Schrift*, 2 vols. (Kampen: Kok, 1966), 1:74).

11

Appendix II
Biblical References to Illumination

This Appendix contains the results of my study of key words related to the Holy Spirit's work of illumining the minds of people throughout the Bible (see Chapter 1 for further explanation). References are listed in canonical order. They are followed by summary explanations and are categorized as either direct or indirect (sometimes by implication) references to illumination.

OLD TESTAMENT REFERENCES

Pentateuch

Genesis 41:38–39 Moses, the author of Genesis, made an early reference to the Spirit of God providing man with discernment and wisdom. Joseph was commended by Pharaoh for possessing this discernment and wisdom, having been gifted to interpret Pharaoh's dreams. This is a direct reference to illumination.

Exodus 31:1–6; 35:30–33 Moses, the author of Exodus, recorded that Bezalel, a son from the tribe of Judah, was filled with the Spirit of God, which enabled him to skillfully and **intelligently** create Israel's tabernacle furniture. This is a direct reference to illumination, as the Spirit of God informs a person's mind to know the LORD's will and how to carry it out.

Numbers 11:16–17, 24–29 Moses, the author of Numbers, recorded how the LORD put some of the Spirit on seventy of the elders of Israel for them to prophesy. The Spirit of God enabled these seventy elders to communicate revelation. This is an indirect reference to illumination by implication because Moses did not record the seventy-understanding revelation in this section.

Numbers 24:1 Moses recorded that Balaam, upon whom the Spirit of God came and gave him an oracle to speak, opened his eyes to see and his ears to hear and understand the message from the LORD. This is a direct reference to illumination, as the Spirit of God opened Balaam's mind to God's Word.

Numbers 27:16–18 Joshua is identified as a man in whom the Spirit of God resides. This, by implication, is an indirect reference to illumination whereby Joshua, by means of the Spirit, could spiritually understand revelation.

Deuteronomy 4:9 Moses, the author of Deuteronomy, exhorted the children of Israel to keep careful watch over their souls, remembering what God had revealed to them. God's revelation of himself, whether by word or deed, was on the heart of the nation Israel. This, by implication, means Israel had been illumined to see God's revelation.

Deuteronomy 17:18–19 Israel's kings wrote and read the Law of God to learn to fear the LORD. This, by implication, is an indirect reference to illumination, and it means that kings were illumined by God's Law to fear the LORD.

Deuteronomy 34:9 Joshua was full of the spirit of wisdom, which implies that he, as the **leader** of Israel, was illumined by the Spirit of God. This is an indirect reference to illumination.

Historical Books

Judges While there is no direct or indirect reference to illumination, a lack of illuminated preachers is indicative of what is known as the darkest days of Israel's history.

1 Samuel 3:7 Samuel had not yet been illumined through the Word of the LORD because it had not been revealed to him up to this point. This is a direct **reference** to illumination.

1 Samuel 10:6, 10 The Spirit of the LORD rushed upon Saul, enabling him to speak prophecies. This is an indirect reference to illumination, by which the Spirit of the LORD enables a person to speak revelation, implying that he can understand revelation.

1 Samuel 19:20–23 The Spirit of God enabled not only Saul but also other prophets to speak revelation. This is an indirect **reference** to illumination, by

which the Spirit of the LORD enables a person to speak revelation, implying that he can understand revelation.

2 Samuel 7:27 David affirms that God has revealed truth to him, and on that basis he was courageous to pray. This is a direct reference to illumination, by which God reveals truth directly to his servant.

2 Samuel 23:1–3 David testified that the Spirit of the LORD spoke to him. Through illumination, David had ready access to know and speak God's Word. This is a direct reference to illumination.

1 Kings 3:9–12; 4:29–32 God granted Solomon's request for understanding, wisdom, and discernment. Solomon's mind was enhanced by the work of God, and he was able to be an effective king over Israel. Solomon was enabled to lead wisely and to write biblical proverbs. This is an indirect reference to illumination where, by implication, the Spirit of God enabled Solomon to understand, be wise, and possess discernment.

1 Kings 22:21–24 God gave a lying spirit to false prophets. This is the antithesis of God's gift of his Spirit to enable understanding and to speak truth. This, by antithesis, is an indirect reference to illumination.

1 Chronicles 12:17–18 The Spirit of the LORD clothed Amasai, empowering him to prophesy. This affirmed the loyalty of the Benjamites and Judahites to David, who was king over Israel. This is an indirect reference to illumination, where, by implication, the Spirit of God enabled men to prophesy God's revelation.

1 Chronicles 22:12 David expresses his deep desire for his son Solomon to be given discretion and understanding as Israel's next king. Solomon's being granted discretion and **understanding** correlates with David's desire for Solomon to obey the Law of the LORD. This is an indirect reference to illumination, where, by implication, the Spirit of God would enable Solomon to understand and be faithful to the Law of the LORD.

1 Chronicles 27:32 Jonathan was affirmed as a man of understanding. This is an indirect reference to illumination as this man's gaining understanding was predicated on the Spirit of God's enabling.

2 Chronicles 18:20–23 A lying spirit given by God to false prophets is the antithesis of God giving his Spirit to enable understanding and speak truth. This, by antithesis, is an indirect reference to illumination.

2 Chronicles 20:14–15 The Spirit of the LORD provided a Levite revelation in the form of prophecy. This is an indirect reference to illumination, where, by implication, Jahaziel was given revelation by the Spirit.

2 Chronicles 24:20 The Spirit of God clothed Zechariah, giving him revelation to prophesy. This is an indirect reference to illumination, in which Zechariah's understanding of the revelation is implied.

2 Chronicles 36:22–23 God stirred up the spirit of Cyrus, which is synonymous to Cyrus being stirred in his mind. This is an indirect reference to illumination, whereby Cyrus was given understanding of revelation to make proclamation and record revelation.

Ezra 1:1–2 God stirred up the spirit of Cyrus, which is synonymous to Cyrus being stirred in his mind. This is an indirect reference to illumination, whereby Cyrus was given understanding of revelation to make proclamation and record revelation.

Nehemiah 8:2–3 When Ezra preached, the ears of Israel were attentive to the Word of the LORD—the Law. This is an indirect reference to illumination; the reference to the people's attentiveness could imply that they were spiritually illumined.

Nehemiah 9:20 Ezra recounted God's faithfulness to Israel in that he gave them his Spirit, enabling them to know revelation. This is a direct reference to illumination.

Nehemiah 9:30 By the Spirit of God, Israel was warned through prophets. They were not given the grace of illumination as they rejected prophetic word. This is an indirect reference to illumination, and specifically the rejection of Spirit-led prophecy.

Nehemiah 10:28 Certain people of Israel—those separated to the Law of God—were characterized by "knowledge and understanding." This is an indirect reference to illumination, the implication being that they were illumined to have "knowledge and understanding."

Wisdom Literature

Job 20:3 Zophar believed he was illumined by "a spirit," but he wasn't. By implication, this is an indirect reference to illumination.

Job 32:7–9 Elihu defined illumination when he attributed his understanding to the "breath of the Almighty." The "breath of the Almighty" is a reference to the Holy Spirit. This is a direct reference to the Holy Spirit.

Job 38:36 The LORD asked a rhetorical question to make the point that he alone gives wisdom and understanding. This is an indirect reference to illumination with no reference to revelation.

Psalm 19:7–8 The Word of God is the agent for illumination. "Enlightening the eyes" implies the spiritual dynamic that takes place in concert with the Word of God. This is a direct reference to illumination.

Psalm 49:3 The psalmist said that meditating will grant understanding. I infer from this that meditating on God's Word provides illumination. This is an indirect reference to illumination, having no reference to the Spirit.

Psalm 51:11 David prayed that the Spirit of God would not be taken from him because of his sin. The Holy Spirit illumined David, providing him with wisdom and discernment to rule as king. This is an indirect reference to illumination, with no reference to the Word of God.

Psalm 82:5 The psalmist described needy people who are without illumination. The reference to "darkness" could imply spiritual darkness or being without illumination. This is an indirect reference to illumination.

Psalm 89:15 The psalmist spoke of a walk of faith that was represented by the knowledge of God. This is an indirect reference to illumination, not specifying the Spirit's work with revelation but rather the effects.

Psalm 111:10 The psalmist said that fearing the LORD is the way to wisdom and understanding. This is an indirect reference to illumination, by implication, and speaks of fearing the LORD, who is revealed by means of the Spirit and the Word of God.

Psalm 119:6 The psalmist could be referring to spiritual eyesight, which implies illumination. This is an indirect reference to illumination, with no mention of the Spirit's work.

Psalm 119:11 The psalmist confessed that he put the Word of God in his heart, which could be understood as means for illumination. This is an indirect reference to illumination, whereby the Word of God was going into the heart by Spirit-wrought faith.

Psalm 119:15–18 The psalmist prayed for illumination, praying that his spiritual eyes would be enabled to spiritually recognize truth from God's Law.

He affirmed his delight in God's Law, and his affections spawned the desire to be illumined by God's Word. This is a direct reference to illumination.

Psalm 119:34–38 The psalmist prayed for understanding, which could be illumination. The result of understanding is obedience. This is an indirect reference to illumination.

Psalm 119:43 The psalmist prayed that the Word of God would be in his speech. The implication could be that the psalmist would continue to be illumined. This could be an indirect reference to illumination.

Psalm 119:73 The psalmist requested understanding, which could be spiritual illumination. This is an indirect reference to illumination, with no mention of the Spirit.

Psalm 119:97–100 The psalmist speaks of the effects experienced from understanding God's Word. This is an indirect reference to illumination, where the psalmist meditates on the Law of God and gains understanding. There is no reference to the Spirit's work in providing understanding.

Psalm 119:103–105 The psalmist made clear that he gained understanding through the Word of God. He characterized the Word of God as a "lamp" and "light," clearly referring to its role as the means of illumining the mind and guiding a person's life. I believe this is a direct reference to illumination, where the Word of God affects a person spiritually as a "lamp" and "light."

Psalm 119:125 The psalmist requested understanding, which could be spiritual illumination. This is an indirect reference to illumination, with no mention of the Spirit.

Psalm 119:130 The psalmist made a declaration that as the Word of God is studied, there is illumination, and understanding is given even for simple-minded people. This is a direct reference to illumination.

Psalm 119:144 The psalmist requested understanding, which could be spiritual illumination. This is an indirect reference to illumination, with no mention of the Spirit.

Psalm 119:169 The psalmist requested understanding, which could be spiritual illumination. This is an indirect reference to illumination, with no mention of the Spirit.

Psalm 139:6–7 The psalmist reveled in the infinite nature of the knowledge of God and yet affirmed the LORD's nearness, citing the presence of his

Spirit. This is an indirect reference by implication. Only a person who is spiritually illumined recognizes God's infinite knowledge and nearness.

Psalm 143:10 The psalmist relied on God's Spirit to lead him. This was in the context of being taught God's will. These statements, understood in apposition, make it reasonable to categorize them under the doctrine of illumination. This is an indirect reference by implication.

Psalm 147:5 The psalmist affirms the Lord's understanding as that which is infinite. Based upon this foundation, God is well qualified to illumine in terms of his right and power. This is an indirect reference to illumination by the implication that God is the source of spiritual illumination.

Proverbs 2:2–3 Solomon, who authored Proverbs, exhorts his readers to seek wisdom and understanding. This is an indirect reference to illumination, without a reference to the Spirit.

Proverbs 2:5–6 Solomon affirmed that the LORD is the source of knowledge. This is an indirect reference to illumination by implication.

Proverbs 3:13 Solomon affirmed the blessing of finding wisdom and understanding. Wisdom and understanding are byproducts of illumination. This is an indirect reference to illumination by implication.

Major Prophets

Isaiah 6:9–10 Isaiah, the author, was called by God as a prophet to preach a message that, for many, would not be understood. This is a reference to the Israelites not being illumined but rather hardened by God's Word. This is an indirect reference to illumination.

Isaiah 11:1–3 Isaiah prophesied of Messiah being illumined by God's Spirit. The "Spirit of wisdom … understanding … [and] knowledge" refers to the dynamic of illumination in the mind of Christ. This is an indirect reference to illumination.

Isaiah 29:10–11 Isaiah speaks of a judgment on Israel in which they are not illumined. The Word of God is being kept from them. This is an indirect reference to illumination.

Isaiah 29:24 Isaiah gave a prophecy that Jerusalem would one day be illumined to understand and believe instruction, which is the Word of God. This is an indirect reference to illumination.

Isaiah 34:16 Isaiah exhorts the nations to read God's Word so they will know what the LORD has commanded and how the Spirit is working. The Word of God is the means by which someone is illumined. This is an indirect reference to illumination.

Isaiah 37:7 As an act of judgment the LORD prompted his enemies in their spirit. This was not being illumined with truth by the Spirit of the LORD.

Isaiah 40:28 Isaiah spoke of God's infinite understanding. God's mind is infinite, so this is not referring to the same kind of understanding involved in human illumination.

Isaiah 42:1–4 Isaiah prophesied of Messiah being illumined by God's Spirit. This is an indirect reference to illumination.

Isaiah 48:16–18 Isaiah, as a prophet, relied on the LORD's Spirit to speak revelation. The LORD, speaking through Isaiah by the Spirit, affirmed his ministry of teaching and guiding. Isaiah, by implication, was illumined by the Spirit, speaking revelation. This is an indirect reference to illumination.

Isaiah 59:21 The LORD, through Isaiah, affirmed his covenant with his people, stating that his Spirit was upon them and that his Word was in their mouths. The Spirit of God enabled the Israelites to have access to God's Word. This is an indirect reference to illumination.

Isaiah 61:1 This was a messianic prophecy that the Spirit of God would empower Christ's ministry. This is an indirect reference to illumination, specifically of the Spirit's role in empowering the Messiah's ministry.

Isaiah 66:2 The LORD, speaking through Isaiah, declares that he will focus on those who are humble toward his Word. This, by implication, indirectly refers to illumination, pointing out how a person's disposition must be humble to be blessed.

Jeremiah 15:16 Jeremiah testifies of how the Word of God became a joy to him. It's possible to infer that the Spirit of God illumined Jeremiah to love his Word.

Jeremiah 31:31–33 Jeremiah prophesies of a day when the LORD will "write" the Word of God on the hearts of his people. This is an indirect reference to illumination, speaking of believers obeying the Word of God by means of transformed hearts.

Ezekiel 2:1–2 Ezekiel testified that the Spirit entered, and, by implication, enabled him to hear God speak to him. This is a direct reference to illumination.

Ezekiel 11:5 At a certain point, the Spirit of the LORD came upon Ezekiel, enabling him to hear God's Word. This is a direct reference to illumination.

Ezekiel 11:19–20 Ezekiel prophesied of God's people being converted by being given a new spirit. Once converted, God's people were enabled to understand and obey his Word. This is an indirect reference to illumination.

Ezekiel 11:24–25 The Spirit of God enabled Ezekiel to see God's revelation. This is an indirect reference to illumination.

Ezekiel 13:3 This was a rebuke to prophets who were not being illumined by God. These prophets, instead of being illumined, looked to themselves for power. This is an indirect reference to illumination.

Ezekiel 36:26–27 Ezekiel prophesied of God's people being converted by being given a new spirit. Once converted, God's people were enabled to understand and obey his Word. This is an indirect reference to illumination.

Ezekiel 37:14–15 The LORD, speaking through Ezekiel, said that his Spirit would enable his people to know him. This is an indirect reference to illumination.

Ezekiel 43:4–7 Ezekiel testified of how the Spirit brought him to a place to hear from the LORD. This, by implication, indirectly refers to illumination; one could infer that the Spirit enabled Ezekiel to hear the Word of God.

Daniel 4:8–9, 18 Nebuchadnezzar affirmed that Daniel was a man indwelt by "the spirit of the holy gods" (which in reality could refer to the Holy Spirit) because he interpreted his dream, which was a revelation from God. This is a direct reference to illumination.

Daniel 5:11–12, 14 Similarly, King Belshazzar affirmed Daniel as a man indwelt by "the spirit of the holy gods" (which in reality could refer to the Holy Spirit) because he interpreted dreams, which were revelations from God. This is a direct reference to illumination.

Daniel 6:3 Again, Daniel was affirmed because he could interpret dreams. This is a direct reference to his gift of illumination.

Daniel 9:21–22 Gabriel was sent to give Daniel understanding. This is not necessarily a reference to illumination, but perhaps the LORD, behind the scenes, illumined Daniel, using Gabriel as a facilitator.

Daniel 10:1 The Word of God was revealed to Daniel, and he understood this revelation and its implications. This is a direct reference to illumination.

Minor Prophets

Hosea 4:10–11 Hosea spoke of how sin blocks understanding or discernment.

Hosea 4:14 Hosea spoke of those without understanding who ruin themselves by their sin. This, by implication, indirectly refers to illumination, pointing out sin's adverse effects regarding it.

Joel 2:28–30 Joel prophesied how the Spirit of God would one day enable men and women to understand revelation. This is an indirect reference to illumination.

Obadiah 7–8 Obadiah condemns those who have rejected the LORD; they are unable to understand, possessing no discernment. This, by implication, indirectly speaks of how sin hinders illumination.

Micah 3:8 Micah spoke of how he was empowered by the Spirit to prophesy. This, by implication, indirectly speaks of illumination.

Zechariah 4:5–6 Zechariah declared that the Word of the LORD came to Zerubbabel by God's Spirit. This is an indirect reference to illumination, whereby the Word is revealed by the Spirit.

Zechariah 7:12 Zechariah spoke of how people hardened their hearts against the Word that was sent by the Spirit. This, by implication, is an indirect reference to illumination. The Word works in concert with the Spirit.

Zechariah 12:10 Zechariah spoke of a "spirit of grace" being poured out on the house of David so that God would be revealed to them. This could be an indirect reference to illumination, depending on whether you understand "spirit of grace" to be God's Spirit or not.

NEW TESTAMENT REFERENCES

Gospels

Matthew 10:20 Jesus commissioned his apostles with confidence that the Spirit would speak through them. This is an indirect reference to illumination, implying that the Spirit who gives revelation also enables understanding.

Matthew 11:15 Jesus made this statement to elicit a response from his hearers. This is an indirect reference to illumination.

Matthew 11:25–26 Jesus thanked the Father for revealing truth to those who followed him. The Father is the one who is noted as revealing truth; I assume this revelation to be by means of the Spirit. This is direct reference to illumination.

Matthew 12:18 The Father put his Spirit upon Jesus to empower his ministry. This, by implication, is an indirect reference to illumination, assuming the Spirit illumined Christ's mind to the revelation he proclaimed.

Matthew 13:13–17 Jesus answered his disciples by telling how Isaiah was called by God to preach a message that would not be understood by many. This is a reference to the Israelites not being illumined but hardened by God's Word. This is an indirect reference to illumination.

Matthew 15:16 Jesus admonished his hearers for not having understanding. This indirectly refers to illumination, illustrating what the hearers did not have.

Matthew 21:42 Jesus quoted a prophetic reference pointing to his crucifixion. This would only be "marvelous" to the "eyes" of those illumined. This, by implication, is an indirect reference to illumination.

Matthew 22:28–29 Jesus rebuked the Pharisees for not knowing the Scriptures or God's power. This, by implication is an indirect reference to illumination; the Word of God and the power of God (possibly a reference to the Spirit of God) going hand in hand.

Matthew 22:43–44 Jesus speaks of David's ability, enabled by the Spirit, to discern Messianic truth. This is a direct reference to illumination.

Mark 7:18 Jesus rebuked the Pharisees for not having understanding. The unbelieving Pharisees were not illumined to grasp spiritual truth. This is an indirect reference to illumination.

Mark 8:17–18 Jesus admonished his hearers for not having understanding. This indirectly refers to illumination, illustrating what the hearers did not have.

Mark 12:36 Jesus speaks of David's ability, enabled by the Spirit, to discern Messianic truth. This is a direct reference to illumination.

Mark 13:11 Jesus commissioned his apostles with the confidence that the Spirit would speak through them. This is an indirect reference to illumination, implying that the Spirit who gives revelation also enables understanding.

Luke 1:15–17 The angel told Zechariah that John the Baptist would be given the Holy Spirit to empower his ministry. This, by implication, is an indirect reference to illumination, assuming that the Spirit illumined John the Baptist and the minds of his hearers to understand the revelation he proclaimed.

Luke 1:67 This, by implication, is an indirect reference to illumination, assuming the Spirit illumined Zechariah and the minds of his hearers to understand the revelation he proclaimed.

Luke 2:25–32 Simeon was illumined by the Spirit to know that he would see the Messiah. Simeon declared the Messiah to be the illumination to the Gentiles. This is a direct reference to illumination.

Luke 4:18 Jesus announced that the Spirit was upon him to empower his ministry of proclamation and healing. This, by implication, is an indirect reference to illumination, assuming the Spirit illumined Christ and his hearers to understand the revelation he proclaimed.

Luke 9:44 Jesus exhorted his hearers to be illumined. This is a direct reference to illumination.

Luke 10:21 Jesus thanked the Father for revealing truth to those who followed him. The Father is the one who is noted as revealing truth; I assume this revelation to be by means of the Spirit. This is a direct reference to illumination.

Luke 12:11–12 Jesus commissioned his apostles with confidence that the Spirit would speak through them. This is an indirect reference to illumination, implying that the Spirit who gives revelation also enables understanding.

Luke 24:24–32 When Jesus preached to two disciples on the road to Emmaus, he rebuked them for not believing. Luke, the author of this account, recorded that later these same two had "their eyes ... opened, and [that] they recognized him." The hearts of these disciples burned within them as Jesus explained the Scriptures concerning himself. This is a direct reference to illumination, where God opens the minds of hearers to spiritually understand truth.

Luke 24:44–49 Luke recorded that, as Christ preached to his disciples, he "opened their minds to understand the Scriptures." This is a direct reference to illumination.

John 1:8–10 John called Jesus the "light, which enlightens." This is an indirect reference to illumination in that Christ and his Word are the significant agents for illumination to take place.

John 2:22 John recorded that after Jesus was raised, his disciples spiritually responded to the Scripture. This is an indirect reference to illumination.

John 4:23–24 Jesus spoke of the internal dynamic that takes place in the spirit of a person when they worship in concert with truth. This, by implication, is an indirect reference to illumination, assuming a believer's spirit is moved by the Holy Spirit to worship.

John 5:39–40 Jesus declared that the "Scriptures … bear witness" about him. This, by implication, is an indirect reference to illumination, assuming a believer, by the Holy Spirit, understands truth.

John 6:63 Jesus taught that the Holy Spirit is the one who grants spiritual life through the agency of his spoken Word. This, by implication, is a direct reference to illumination, in that it takes place through the agency of the Spirit and the teachings of Christ.

John 14:17 Jesus taught that the "Spirit of truth" (a reference to the Holy Spirit) is not received by the sinful world, because the world does not know him. Jesus affirmed that his true disciples know the "Spirit of truth" because he resides in them. This is an indirect reference to illumination.

John 14:26 Jesus said to his disciples that the Holy Spirit would teach them and bring truth back to their minds. This is a direct reference to the work of illumination.

John 15:26–16:1 Jesus said to his disciples that the Holy Spirit would teach them and bring truth back to their minds and that they would be empowered to "bear witness" about Christ. This is a direct reference to the work of illumination.

John 16:12–15 Jesus said to his disciples that the Holy Spirit would guide them. By virtue of the Spirit being designated the "Spirit of truth," this is an indirect reference to the Spirit's role in illumination.

Church History

Acts 1:2 Luke, the author of Acts, recorded that Jesus taught by means of the Holy Spirit. This, by implication, indirectly refers to illumination in that the Holy Spirit is the means by which Christ's teaching would be received and understood.

Acts 2:4 Luke recorded that the Spirit of God gave the disciples revelation to speak. This, by implication, indirectly refers to illumination.

Acts 2:17–19 Peter quoted Joel prophesying that the Spirit of God would one day enable men and women to prophesy and understand revelation. This is an indirect reference to illumination.

Acts 2:33 Peter preached that the Holy Spirit had enabled his hearers to spiritually see and hear truth. This is a direct reference to illumination.

Acts 4:25 Peter preached that David was enabled to prophesy by means of the Spirit. This, by implication, is an indirect reference to illumination.

Acts 4:31 Luke records how the early church, "filled with the Holy Spirit," spoke the Word of God. This is an indirect reference to illumination, assuming these believers, by the Spirit, had understanding of the revelation they were speaking.

Acts 5:3 By asking why Ananias lied to the Holy Spirit, Peter might have been implying that Ananias had the opportunity to be illumined by the Spirit. This is an indirect reference to illumination.

Acts 5:9 By asking why Sapphira tested Spirit, Peter might have been implying that Sapphira had the opportunity to be illumined by the Spirit. This could be an indirect reference to illumination.

Acts 5:32 Peter declared that the Holy Spirit is given to believers who obey God. This, by implication, is an indirect reference to illumination, in that obedience is spawned by understanding revelation.

Acts 7:51 Stephen condemned the crowd for not being illumined. This is a direct reference to illumination.

Acts 7:57 Luke recorded that the crowds plugged their ears, which could be a physical expression that they were not illumined. This, by implication, is an indirect reference to illumination.

Acts 8:29–31 Philip inquired of the Ethiopian as to whether or not he understood, which could be taken as a reference to illumination. This, by implication, is an indirect reference to illumination.

Acts 9:3–5 Luke records Saul's conversion, in which he was spiritually illumined by Christ. This is a direct reference to illumination.

Acts 10:44–47 Luke records that Gentile believers believed by the Spirit and manifested revelation by speaking in tongues. This, by implication, is an indirect reference to illumination.

Acts 11:12–17 Luke records that Gentile believers believed by means of the Spirit, being baptized by the Spirit. This, by implication, is an indirect reference to illumination.

Acts 11:28 Agabus was given revelation by the Spirit. This, by implication, is an indirect reference to illumination.

Acts 13:2–4 The Holy Spirit spoke to the early church, giving direct revelation. This, by implication, is an indirect reference to illumination.

Acts 15:28 The apostles at the Jerusalem council affirmed the direction the Holy Spirit gave to them. This, by implication, is an indirect reference to illumination.

Acts 16:6–7 The Spirit directed Paul and Silas on their missionary journey. This, by implication, is an indirect reference to illumination.

Acts 17:20 Paul preached in Athens to some who were not illumined and who were calling the truth strange. This, by implication, is an indirect reference to illumination.

Acts 18:25 Paul preached with fervency "in spirit," believing his message in earnest. This, by implication, is an indirect reference to illumination.

Acts 19:6 Luke records that Paul had preached to disciples of John who believed by means of the Spirit and were being baptized by the Spirit. This, by implication, is an indirect reference to illumination manifesting revelatory gifts.

Acts 19:21 The Spirit directed Paul to back to Jerusalem, and then ultimately to Rome. This, by implication, is an indirect reference to illumination.

Acts 21:4 The disciples, illumined by the Spirit, warned Paul not to go to Jerusalem. This is a direct reference to illumination.

Acts 21:11 Agabus, by the Spirit, spoke revelation concerning Paul's destination. This, by implication, is an indirect reference to illumination.

Acts 22:6–11 As a prisoner, Paul testified concerning his conversion to the mob in Jerusalem. He described his conversion as being spiritually illumined by the Lord. This is a direct reference to illumination.

Acts 22:17–18 Paul fell into a trance and saw the Lord Jesus directly giving him revelation. This, by implication, is an indirect reference to illumination.

Acts 26:12–18 Paul testified to King Agrippa of his conversion whereby he was spiritually illumined by the Lord. The Lord Jesus commissioned Paul to be a witness to the Gentiles so that they too would be illumined. This is a direct reference to illumination.

Acts 28:25–27 Paul preached in Rome and quoted Isaiah 6:9 as a condemnation of people unable to spiritually discern truth. This is an indirect reference to illumination in that some were not illumined to spiritually see or hear truth.

Epistles

Romans 1:16–17 Paul declared that the gospel is the power for salvation for those who believe. Within the gospel, the righteousness of God is revealed. This is a direct reference to illumination wherein the gospel reveals God's righteousness.

Romans 8:4–11 Paul taught the believer to be spiritually minded. This, by implication, is an indirect reference to illumination.

Romans 8:13–16 Paul taught that believers receive, by the Spirit, the assurance that they are adopted as children of God. By the illumination of the Holy Spirit, a believer's spirit or inner man resonates with the Holy Spirit, bringing assurance of salvation and confidence in his or her relationship to God. This is a direct reference to the doctrine of illumination.

Romans 8:26–27 Paul describes the spiritual dynamic between the believer's weakness and the intercessory ministry of the Holy Spirit. The Spirit of God aligns the believer's prayers with the will of God. This, by implication, is an indirect reference to illumination.

Romans 9:1 Paul testified that he was telling the truth by the illuminating Holy Spirit. This is a direct reference to the doctrine of illumination.

Romans 10:14–18 Paul taught that faith comes from hearing the Word of Christ. This, by implication, is an indirect reference to illumination.

Romans 11:8 Paul taught that the Jews, being under God's judgment, were rendered unable to see or hear truth. This is the opposite of being illumined by the Spirit to perceive truth. This, by implication, is an indirect reference to illumination.

Romans 15:13 Paul gave a doxology to the church, speaking of the Holy Spirit's power to fill believers with hope. This is an indirect reference to illumination.

Romans 16:25–26 Paul taught that the gospel is a revelation of something that was hidden before but is now known to the nations. This, by implication, is an indirect reference to illumination.

1 Corinthians 2:4 Paul reported that his preaching was a demonstration of the Spirit. To comprehend his preaching; one must be illumined by the Spirit. This, by implication, is an indirect reference to illumination.

1 Corinthians 2:9–16 Paul taught that the way to comprehend spiritual truth is by the Spirit of God. He taught that the Spirit of God is the only Being credentialed by his knowledge of God to illumine the mind of man. This is a direct reference to the doctrine of illumination.

1 Corinthians 12:3 Paul taught that a person speaking by the Holy Spirit cannot curse Jesus, and a person cannot praise Jesus except by the Holy Spirit. He taught that praising or cursing the Lord had to do with whether a person was illumined by the Spirit or not. This, by implication, is an indirect reference to the doctrine of illumination.

1 Corinthians 12:4–8, 10–12 Paul taught that spiritual gifts are given through the Spirit, and that particular gifts are revelatory. These gifts are related to the doctrine of illumination in that one gifted in this way knows revelation by means of the Spirit.

1 Corinthians 13:2 Paul taught that it was essential to possess love, no matter a person's spiritual giftedness. This, by implication, is an indirect reference to the doctrine of illumination.

1 Corinthians 13:9–12 Paul taught that full knowledge is for those who are glorified. This, by implication, is an indirect reference to the doctrine of illumination.

1 Corinthians 14:6, 12–16, 26–30 Paul taught that it was unfruitful to use one's prophetic gift if it was unintelligible or devoid of knowledge. He taught that revelation must have content. This, by implication, is an indirect reference to the doctrine of illumination.

2 Corinthians 3:3–9 Paul taught that the church possesses a ministry of the Spirit. He implied by this that new-covenant believers have been illumined by the Holy Spirit. This, by implication, is an indirect reference to the doctrine of illumination.

2 Corinthians 3:17–18 Paul taught that believers were illumined by the Spirit of God to behold "the glory of the Lord." Such believers were being transformed in holiness. This is a direct reference to the doctrine of illumination.

2 Corinthians 4:2–6 Paul taught that the gospel is veiled to those who do not believe. He also taught that by hearing Christ proclaimed, a person can be illumined to belief—to seeing the glory of Christ by faith. This is a direct reference to the doctrine of illumination.

2 Corinthians 4:13 Paul taught that belief is initiated by preaching. Belief is predicated on illumination. This, by implication, is an indirect reference to the doctrine of illumination.

Galatians 1:11–12 Paul taught that he received the gospel through a revelation of Jesus Christ. He was illumined by God to believe. This is an indirect reference to the doctrine of illumination.

Galatians 2:2 Paul testified that he had been given a revelation of the gospel by God. This is an indirect reference to the doctrine of illumination.

Galatians 3:2–5 Paul taught that God supplied the Spirit to the church. This is an indirect reference to the doctrine of illumination.

Galatians 3:14 Paul taught that all who receive the Spirit do so through faith. This is an indirect reference to the doctrine of illumination.

Galatians 4:6 Paul affirmed that believers are given confidence in their sonship by means of the Holy Spirit. This is a direct reference to the doctrine of illumination.

Galatians 5:5 Paul taught that, by the Spirit and by believing, believers anticipate heaven. This is an indirect reference to the doctrine of illumination.

Ephesians 1:13–14 Paul taught that believers are given the Holy Spirit as a guarantee of their salvation. By the Spirit's illumination, believers know they are promised salvation. This is an indirect reference to the doctrine of illumination.

Ephesians 1:17–18 Paul taught that because believers are regenerate, they can be illumined to greater spiritual realities. This is a direct reference to the doctrine of illumination.

Ephesians 2:18 Paul taught that believers have access to the Father by means of the Spirit. This is an indirect reference to the doctrine of illumination.

Ephesians 3:3 Paul testified that the mystery of the gospel was made known to him by revelation. This is a direct reference to the doctrine of illumination.

Ephesians 3:4–5 Paul testified that the mystery of the gospel was made known to him by revelation. This is a direct reference to the doctrine of illumination.

Ephesians 3:16–21 Paul prayed for the Ephesians to be illumined by the power of God to know the love of Christ. This is a direct reference to the doctrine of illumination.

Ephesians 4:18 Paul referred to unbelievers as those without illumined minds. This is an indirect reference to the doctrine of illumination.

Ephesians 4:22–23 Paul taught that believers are to have renewed minds through the knowledge of Christ. This is an indirect reference to the doctrine of illumination.

Ephesians 5:9–10 Paul taught that believers must possess discernment that is based on righteous living. This is an indirect reference to the doctrine of illumination.

Ephesians 5:17–18 Paul taught that believers are to pursue God's will, avoid returning to party-living, and allow themselves to be illumined by the Holy Spirit. This is a direct reference to the doctrine of illumination.

Ephesians 6:17–19 When Paul described the spiritual weapon of "the sword of the Spirit," he was teaching that the Spirit of God is inextricably linked to the Word of God. This, by implication, is an indirect reference to the doctrine of illumination.

Philippians 1:8–9 Paul desired that the believers in this church would grow in their spiritual knowledge and spiritual discernment. This is an indirect reference to the doctrine of illumination.

Philippians 3:3 Paul defined believers as those who worship by means of the Spirit of God. Only believers illumined by the Spirit worship by the Spirit. This is an indirect reference to the doctrine of illumination.

Colossians 1:4–6 Paul taught that believers, by grace, first have to come to an understanding of the truth. This is an indirect reference to the doctrine of illumination.

Colossians 1:9–10 Paul prayed that these believers would be illumined by the truth and would grow both in knowledge and in pleasing the Lord. This is a direct reference to the doctrine of illumination.

Colossians 1:12–13 Paul described Christianity as a deliverance from darkness to light. This is an indirect reference to the doctrine of illumination.

Colossians 2:2–3 Paul's desire was for these believers, by illumination, to gain clear knowledge and assurance from the gospel. This is a direct reference to the doctrine of illumination.

Colossians 3:10 Paul taught that spiritual renewal comes by means of knowledge. This is an indirect reference to the doctrine of illumination.

Colossians 3:16 Paul desired for the teachings of Christ to be deeply rooted in the hearts of these believers so as to produce spiritual wisdom and spiritual responses. This is a direct reference to the doctrine of illumination.

1 Thessalonians 1:4–6 Paul affirmed these believers' salvation based upon the way the gospel was empowered by the Spirit. This is an indirect reference to the doctrine of illumination.

1 Thessalonians 2:13 Paul affirmed these believers as those who received their message, preached by Paul and others, as actually being God's Word. He also affirmed that the Word of God works in believers. This, by implication, is an indirect reference to the doctrine of illumination.

1 Thessalonians 4:6–8 Paul taught that to disregard obedience is to disregard conviction by the Holy Spirit. This, by implication, is an indirect reference to

the doctrine of illumination because the Spirit of God illumines a person regarding his or her sin.

1 Thessalonians 5:18–20 Paul taught that believers can quench or remove the effect of the Spirit within a worship setting. This, by implication, is an indirect reference to the doctrine of illumination, because the Spirit is the one who enlightens the Scripture in a person's mind, and this verse speaks of the effectiveness of illumination.

2 Thessalonians 2:13 Paul taught that sanctification by means of the Spirit and believing in the truth go hand in hand. This is an indirect reference to illumination.

1 Timothy 2:4 Paul taught that when a person is saved, he or she is illumined—able to know the truth. This is a direct reference to illumination.

2 Timothy 1:14 Paul taught that the Holy Spirit is the agent by which leaders in the church are enabled to discern how to guard the gospel. This is an indirect reference to illumination.

2 Timothy 2:7 Paul exhorted Timothy to think about what he had just taught, on the assumption that the Lord would illumine his mind to understand the truth. This is a direct reference to illumination.

2 Timothy 2:25 Paul taught that correcting opponents could facilitate repentance and then illumination to know the truth. This is a direct reference to illumination.

2 Timothy 3:7 Paul taught that false teachers learn but are never illumined. This is an indirect reference to illumination.

2 Timothy 3:15–16 Paul reminded Timothy of the Scripture's power and how it enabled Timothy to gain the wisdom for salvation. This is an indirect reference to illumination.

Titus 1:1 Paul acknowledged the believers under Titus's ministry as those who possessed "knowledge of the truth." This was more than intellectual knowledge; it was illumined knowledge of inspired Scripture. This is an indirect reference to illumination.

Hebrews 3:7–8 The author of Hebrews quoted Psalm 95:7–11 to warn his hearers not to harden their hearts. He stated that the Holy Spirit was saying this to this church and that this was an example of how God's Word was shared for the purpose of spiritual illumination. This, by implication, is an indirect reference to illumination.

Hebrews 4:12 The author of Hebrews described the dynamic convicting ministry of the Word of God in the believer's heart. This, by implication, is an indirect reference to illumination, showing that believers are enlightened regarding their sin.

Hebrews 6:4–6 The author of Hebrews warned the church that a person exposed to the power of God can experience levels of spiritual enlightenment by the Holy Spirit which, if rejected, will harden the heart. This enlightenment is not the illumination a believer receives, because the receptor is still in darkness; instead of believing truth, the person rejects truth. This is an indirect reference to illumination.

Hebrews 9:8 The author of Hebrews explained that the Holy Spirit had made known information regarding old covenant tabernacle worship. This, by implication, is an indirect reference to illumination.

Hebrews 10:15–17 The author of Hebrews indicated that the Holy Spirit had illumined Jeremiah 31:33 to him so that he could apply it in a new covenant context. This is a direct reference to illumination.

Hebrews 10:26 The author of Hebrews warned the church that a person who receives spiritual knowledge of the truth and rejects it will be rejected by God. Such a person has not received this knowledge by faith and is not truly illumined. This is an indirect reference to illumination.

James 1:18 James made it clear that the vehicle for spiritual birth is by means of the Scripture. This is an indirect reference to illumination.

James 1:23–25 James made it clear that a person who genuinely hears the Word of God responds to the Word of God. This, by implication, is an indirect reference to illumination.

James 3:13 James asked this rhetorical question regarding the spiritual status of those in the church. He indicated that a person who is characteristically wise or possesses understanding will show it by a lifestyle of humility and discernment. This, by implication, is an indirect reference to illumination.

James 4:5 James asked this rhetorical question so the church would recognize that a person who loves the world loses his or her spiritual intimacy with God. This, by implication, is an indirect reference to illumination.

1 Peter 1:10–12 Peter wrote to the church that the prophets, by the Spirit, had some indication of the salvation that their Messiah would bring. This is a direct reference to the doctrine of illumination.

1 Peter 1:13 Peter exhorted the church to prepare their minds for Christ to be revealed at his return. Peter identified the unique way Christ will be revealed to believers when he returns. This is an indirect reference to the doctrine of illumination.

1 Peter 1:23 Peter made it clear that the vehicle for spiritual birth is Scripture. This is an indirect reference to the doctrine of illumination.

1 Peter 2:2–3 Peter taught that believers taste the Word of God. This could be a reference to the spiritual dynamic that takes place when a person is illumined by the Scripture. This is an indirect reference to the doctrine of illumination.

2 Peter 1:3 Peter wrote that God's sanctifying power comes through the knowledge of God. This is an indirect reference to the doctrine of illumination.

2 Peter 1:15–21 Peter affirmed that Scripture, rather than spiritual experience, is the means of illumination. This is a direct reference to the doctrine of illumination.

2 Peter 2:20 Peter affirmed that God's power for sanctification comes through the knowledge of God. This is an indirect reference to illumination.

2 Peter 3:15–16 Peter affirmed that Paul's writings were given to him through wisdom, which refers to the inspiration of the Holy Spirit (see 2 Tim. 3:16). This is an indirect reference to illumination.

2 Peter 3:18 Peter wrote that God's power for sanctification comes through growing in knowledge of God. This is an indirect reference to illumination.

1 John 2:8 John referred to the light that has come with the coming of Christ. Believers are illumined by the light of the gospel. This is an indirect reference to illumination.

1 John 2:20, 27 John affirmed that believers can understand truth because of their anointing from the Holy Spirit. This is a direct reference to illumination.

1 John 3:24 John taught that the Spirit of God brings assurance to true believers. This is an indirect reference to illumination.

1 John 4:1–6 John taught that true believers have spiritual discernment and are able to tell the difference between the truth and error. The genuine believer "listens" to truth. This is an indirect reference to illumination.

1 John 4:13 John taught that the Spirit of God brings assurance to true believers. This is an indirect reference to illumination.

1 John 5:6–11 John taught that the Spirit and the truth are inextricably linked. He taught that the Spirit of God brings assurance to true believers. The "testimony" is a direct reference to illumination.

1 John 5:20 John taught that the Spirit of God brings assurance to true believers. The "understanding" that a believer has is an indirect reference to illumination.

Jude 20 Jude exhorted believers to pray by means of the Holy Spirit. This, by implication, is an indirect reference to illumination.

Prophecy

Revelation 1:1 John testified that Jesus was revealed to him in a vision. This revelation is, by implication, an indirect reference to illumination.

Revelation 1:3 John affirmed believers who are able to hear this prophecy, which is truth. Hearing could be a reference to illumination. This is an indirect reference to illumination.

Revelation 1:10 John affirmed that he was able to hear this prophecy, which is truth. Hearing was illumination. This is a direct reference to illumination.

Revelation 2:7, 11, 17, 29; 3:1, 6, 13 John exhorted believers to be open to hearing from the Spirit of God, who was directly connected to the prophecy John was writing. This is an indirect reference to the doctrine of illumination.

Revelation 4:1–2 John testified to being caught up in a vision by the Holy Spirit. This, by implication, is an indirect reference to the doctrine of illumination.

Revelation 19:10 John referred to the spiritual nature of the truth. This, by implication, has indirect bearing on the doctrine of illumination.

Revelation 21:10 John testified that he was shown this prophecy by means of the Spirit. This, by implication, is an indirect reference to the doctrine of illumination.

Revelation 22:17 The Spirit of God calls believers to believe. Genuine believers will spiritually thirst for the truth. This is an indirect reference to the doctrine of illumination.

Revelation 22:18–19 John warned those who might hear and reject truth by adding to it or taking away from it. Hearing and not believing brings condemnation. This is an indirect reference to the doctrine of illumination, as it describes the opposite.

Conclusion

As the research reflects, the doctrine of illumination spans the Scriptures. My conclusion is that God has clearly spoken regarding the way in which he opens the minds of people to his Word. I see four categories into which these scriptural references fall regarding the role of illumination:

- **Condemnation**, referring to the person who is without illumination and is rejecting the Word of God.
- **Conversion**, speaking of the transformation that takes place when God changes a heart and gives illumination.
- **Communication**, speaking of how prophets, preachers, and evangelists are illumined to preach God's Word, and how hearers are illumined by the preaching of God's Word.
- **Convictions**, which are gained as believers are enriched in their own spiritual walks, acquiring greater certainty and affection over spiritual truth as they are illumined by the Spirit and his Word.

Bibliography

Anderson, Kent, Review of Craddock, As One Without Authority, at: preaching.org.

————Review of Doug Pagitt, Preaching Re-Imagined, at: preaching.org.

Averbeck, Richard E., "God, People, and the Bible: The Relationship between Illumination and Biblical Scholarship," in Wallace, Daniel B., and Sawyer M. James, eds., Who's Afraid of the Holy Spirit? An Investigation into the Ministry of the Spirit of God Today (Dallas: Biblical Studies Press, 2005).

Bergen, Robert D., 1, 2 Samuel, vol. 7, New American Commentary (Nashville: B & H Publishers, 1996).

Berkhof, Hendrikus, The Doctrine of the Holy Spirit: The Annie Kinkead Warfield Lectures, 1963–1964 (Richmond, VA: John Knox Press, 1964).

BibleWorks 6: Software for Biblical Exegesis and Research, CD-ROM (Norfolk, VA: BibleWorks, LLC, 2005).

Block, Daniel I., Judges, Ruth, vol. 6, New American Commentary (Nashville: B & H Publishers, 1999).

Calvin, John, Calvin: Institutes of the Christian Religion, vols. xx and xxi of Baillie, John, McNeill, John T., and Van Dusen, Henry P., eds., The Library of Christian Classics (Louisville, KY: Westminster John Knox Press, 1960).

————and Parker, T. H. L., tr., The Epistles of Paul the Apostle to the Galatians, Ephesians, Philippians and Colossians, vol. ii of Torrance, David W., and Torrance, Thomas F., eds., Calvin's New Testament Commentaries (Grand Rapids: Eerdmans, 1965).

————"Geneva Catechism," in Torrance, Thomas F., ed. and tr., The School of Faith: The Catechisms of the Reformed Church (Eugene, OR: Wipf and Stock, 1959).

————and Beveridge, Henry, tr., Tracts and Treatises on the Doctrine and Worship of the Church (Grand Rapids: Eerdmans, 1849; 1958).

Craddock, Fred B., As One Without Authority (St. Louis, MI: Chalice Press, 2001).

———"Preaching: An Appeal to Memory," in Graves, Mike, ed., What's the Matter with Preaching Today? (Louisville, KY: Westminster John Knox Press, 2004).

Dillenberger, John, ed., Introduction, John Calvin: Selections from his Writings (Scholars Press for the American Academy of Religion, 1975).

Dorsey, David A., The Literary Structure of the Old Testament: A Commentary on Genesis–Malachi (Grand Rapids: Baker Academic, 1999).

Edwards, Jonathan, The Religious Affections (Carlisle, PA: Banner of Truth, 1746; 1986)

Farris, Stephen, review of Craddock, As One Without Authority, in Homiletic, 27/1 (2002), pp. 35–36.

Garland, David E., Luke, Zondervan Exegetical Commentary on the New Testament (Grand Rapids: Zondervan, 2011).

Hargrove, Carl A., "The Role of the Holy Spirit as Convictor and Supporter in Preaching," (ThM Thesis, The Master's Seminary, 2006).

Heisler, Greg, Spirit-Led Preaching: The Holy Spirit's Role in Sermon Preparation and Delivery (Nashville: B & H Academic, 2007).

Hodge, Charles, Commentary on the Second Epistle to the Corinthians (Grand Rapids: Eerdmans, 1864; n.d.).

———Ephesians, The Geneva Series of Commentaries (Carlisle, PA: Banner of Truth, 1856; 1991).

Hoehner, Harold, Ephesians: An Exegetical Commentary (Grand Rapids: Baker Academic, 2002).

Kaiser, Walter, "The Power of the Word of God," sermon preached at The Bible Church of Little Rock, October 22, 2006, at: http://64.19.50.210/Default.aspx.

Kent, Homer A., Jr., Ephesians: The Glory of the Church, Everyman's Bible Commentary (Chicago: Moody Press, 1971).

Kierkegaard, Søren, and Hong, Howard V., and Hong, Edna H., trs. and eds., For Self- Examination in Kierkegaard's Writings, vol. xxi (Princeton: Princeton University Press, 1851; 1990).

Larsen, David L., The Company of Preachers: A History of Biblical Preaching from the Old Testament to the Modern Era (Grand Rapids Kregel, 1998).

Lawson, Steven J., The Daring Mission of William Tyndale, First ed., A Long Line of Godly Men Profile (Orlando, FL: Reformation Trust, 2015).

Lloyd-Jones, D. Martyn, Preaching and Preachers (London: Hodder and Stoughton, 1971; 1985).

Longman III, Tremper, "1 Samuel," in The Expositor's Bible Commentary, Rev. ed. (Grand Rapids: Zondervan, 1996).

Longman III, Tremper, and Garland, David E., 1 Samuel–2 Kings, The Expositor's Bible Commentary (Grand Rapids: Zondervan, 2009).

MacArthur, John, and Mayhue, Richard, Biblical Doctrine: A Systematic Summary of Bible Truth (Wheaton, IL: Crossway, 2017).

Mohler, Albert, "Why Do We Preach? A Foundation for Christian Preaching, Part One," December 15, 2005, "Commentary," at: AlbertMohler.com.

Mueller, J. Theodore, "The Holy Spirit and the Scriptures," in Henry, Carl F. H., ed., Revelation and the Bible: Contemporary Evangelical Thought (Grand Rapids: Baker, 1958).

Nichols, Stephen J., An Absolute Sort of Certainty: The Holy Spirit and the Apologetics of Jonathan Edwards (Phillipsburg, NJ: P & R, 2003).

Oswalt, John, The Holy One of Israel (Eugene, OR: Wipf and Stock Publishers, 2014).

Owen, John, The Holy Spirit: His Gifts and Power (Grand Rapids: Kregel, 1954).

————and Goold, William H., ed., The Works of John Owen, vol. iv (London: Banner of Truth, 1850; 1967).

Ownes, R. Eugene, review of Fred Craddock, "As One Without Authority," in Perspectives in Religious Studies, 7/3 (1980), pp. 246–247.

Pache, René, and Needham, Helen I., tr., The Inspiration and Authority of Scripture (Salem, WI: Sheffield Publishing, 1969; 1992).

Packer, J. I., "Calvin the Theologian," in Duffield, G. E., ed., John Calvin: A Collection of Essays (London: Sutton Courtenay Press, 1966).

———God Has Spoken (Grand Rapids: Baker, 1988).

Pagitt, Doug, Preaching Re-Imagined: The Role of the Sermon in Communities of Faith (Grand Rapids: Zondervan, 2005).

Pascal, Blaise, and Trotter, W. F., tr., Pensées, (New York: Random House, 1941).

Piper, John, "The Divine Majesty of the Word: John Calvin, The Man and His Preaching," Bethlehem Conference for Pastors, February 4, 1997.

———Seeing and Savoring Jesus Christ (Wheaton, IL: Crossway, 2004).

Ramm, Bernard L., Rapping about the Spirit (Waco, TX: Word, 1974).

Reid, Robert Stephen, "Preaching Re-Imagined: The Role of the Sermon in Communities of Faith," in The Christian Century, August 22, 2006.

Ridderbos, Herman, and de Witt, John Richard, tr., Paul: An Outline of his Theology (Grand Rapids: Eerdmans, 1966; 1975,).

Rowell, Andy, "Review of Preaching Re-Imagined by Doug Pagitt," Church Leadership Conversations, February 26, 2006, at: andyrowell.net.

Ruppert, L., "ארץ," in G. Johannes Botterweck, Helmer Ringgren, and Heinz-Josef Fabry, eds., Green , David E., tr., Theological Dictionary of the Old Testament (Grand Rapids; Cambridge: Eerdmans, 1998).

Sandy, D. Brent, and Giese, Jr., Ronald L., eds., Cracking Old Testament Codes (Nashville: B & H Publishers, 1995).

Shivers, Mark, "Preaching Re-Imagined: A Review," at: theOoze.com.

Sproul, R. C., "The Internal Testimony of the Holy Spirit," in Geisler, Norman L., ed., Inerrancy (Grand Rapids: Zondervan, 1980).

Tsumura, David Toshio, The First Book of Samuel, New International Commentary on the Old Testament (Grand Rapids: Eerdmans, 2007).

Tyndale, William, The Prologue from the Cologne Quarto (1525).

Vanhoozer, Kevin J., Is There a Meaning in This Text? The Bible, the Reader, and the Morality of Literary Knowledge (Grand Rapids: Zondervan, 1998).

Varner, William, To Preach or Not to Preach (CreateSpace Independent Publishing Platform: 2018).

Warfield, B. B., Calvin and Augustine (Philadelphia: P & R, 1980, 1956; 1980).

Zemek, George J., The Word of God in the Child of God: Exegetical, Theological, and Homiletical Reflections from the 119th Psalm (Mango, FL: n.p.; n.d.).

www.ingramcontent.com/pod-product-compliance
Lightning Source LLC
La Vergne TN
LVHW051241080426
835513LV00016B/1707